Programs for Parish Councils

Programs for Parish Councils

AN ACTION MANUAL

Bernard Lyons

Introduction by
Mr. and Mrs. Patrick F. Crowley

© 1972
CLARETIAN PUBLICATIONS • Chicago, Illinois

Copyright © 1969 by Bernard Lyons

Excerpts from *The Jerusalem Bible* copyright © 1966 by Darton, Longman and Todd, Ltd., and Doubleday and Company, Inc. Used by permission of the publishers.

Excerpts from *The Documents of Vatican II,* published by Guild Press, Association Press, America Press, and Herder and Herder, and copyrighted © 1966 by The America Press. Used by permission of the publishers.

Standard Book Number 87298-110-X
Library of Congress Catalog Card Number 69-20417
Second printing, April 1969

Printed in the United States of America.

With love, to Ed and Barbara Lyons
and their children

Introduction

WHAT we like best about Bernard Lyons' *Programs for Parish Councils* is that it does not seek to tell the reader about what he knows best—*his* parish. It is an action book, one that will enable the reader (especially if he is working within a group) to ask the kinds of questions that will lead to action. The author poses the questions against a background of Vatican II theology and general discussion of parish life. But eventually it is the reader who must act and continue to act. This book will help to show him the way.

We would add but a few comments to what Bernard Lyons says in his book. As persons who have devoted the past quarter-century to the Christian Family Movement, we are committed to the idea of action. We do not ask action for its own sake. Nor do we mean to downgrade the large value of discussion, study, and contemplation. But the author would be among the first to agree that there are more far-ranging discussions of parish life than are contained in this book. He does not intend the book as a stimulator of discussion so much as a guideline to action.

We would not imply, however, that the book is without a point of view. Clearly, it is there; it is implicit in virtually every paragraph. It is this: The parish of the future, in whatever form it may eventually take, will of necessity demand that its members have—there is no way of avoiding the vogue phrase—a "piece of the action." That is where its future lies; that is the stance that will lead to the changed structures we may now see only dimly.

What could be more up-to-date? And what could be older? For we know that Christ was the kind of gentle revolutionary who demanded of people that they give of themselves. Christ was a person who asked favors. He involved people. He gave them a piece of the action. He did so because as persons they had the right to a freedom that would help them to know themselves and to advance their own personhood.

Would it be exaggerating things too much to say that the problems of our parishes today are not too different from the problems of our world? Our urban world has lead to depersonalization; we seem to be lost in numbers. The automobile has taken us out of the home (and away from the parish) while the television set has brought us back (and kept us away from parish activities). If we are able to shop quickly by using a shopping center with its familiar mass of concrete surrounding it, so too must we leave church quickly on Sunday to make room for cars coming in for the next Mass. As we drive bumper-to-bumper on our amazingly new (and overcrowded) expressways we may sometimes be attacked by the suspicion that we are engaged in a symbolic dumb show of modern life—each of us enclosed in a small cubicle resting on our share of asphalt, crowded beyond endurance, unable to move forward. On the highway we are very close to each other and yet so far—silently imprisoned by our preoccupation, unable to communicate with each other.

So too with our parishes. They are large and getting

INTRODUCTION

larger. We stand next to strangers at Mass, wondering who they might be. People come and go, move in and out of the parish; a ten-year resident is regarded as an old-timer. We wave hello to the assistant pastor, who is rushing toward the basement church-hall to help in the distribution of Communion, as we ourselves dash for the parking lot. We remind ourselves that it seems ages since we attended a meeting in the parish. We know that the debt is large (and getting larger) and that the school is having a tough time raising salaries for its teachers. We remind ourselves that maybe one of these days we must pitch in and help, but, somehow, like being stranded on the expressway, there are just too many things to do, too many voices, too many distracting influences, and we don't really know how to begin.

That's what this book is about—how to begin. And how to continue.

The author uses the celebrated observe-judge-act technique pioneered by the late Cardinal Cardijn and used for this past quarter-century by members of the specialized Catholic Action movements—the Christian Family Movement, the Young Christian Students, and the Young Christian Movement. We can attest that this formula for action works. It works best when it is used with others. When friends and neighbors, and in this case *parishioners* as well, meet to *see* their parish, *judge* its goals, its history, the impediments that stand in the way of its helping the people of God, and then *act* upon their reasoned, considered judgment—then it is that they will be on the road, we have found, to action that will be satisfying and permanent.

With these few observations, we offer our prayers and best wishes that this book will be a guide to successful action to all who read and use it.

PAT AND PATTY CROWLEY

Contents

Introduction
Mr. and Mrs. Patrick F. Crowley   vii

The Use of This Book   xiii

1. THE WORSHIPPING COMMUNITY   1
2. CHRISTIAN FORMATION   15
3. THE PARISH COUNCIL   21
4. COUNCIL COMMITTEES   31
   Action Meetings for Committees
5. WORSHIP   41
6. COMMUNITY LIFE   53
7. EDUCATION   65
8. APOSTOLATE   77
9. FAMILY LIFE   89
10. SOCIAL   101
11. FINANCE AND ADMINISTRATION   113

The Use of This Book

UNLIKE most books, which are designed to be read by one person at a time for that person's enjoyment and/or increase in knowledge, this book is written to help the reader act—and act in concert with his fellow-members in a worshipping community. There is a sense of satisfaction, of completion, in reading most books, in one or more sittings, to the final page. Hopefully, this book will leave you dissatisfied if you try to use it in that manner.

This book will serve you and its purposes well if it motivates you to talk with your fellow parishioners, with your neighbors, and with the people with whom you work, live, and come briefly into contact in your daily life; if it moves you to reflect on these conversations and to discover the needs and wants of the people around you; and if it inspires you to tell the persons around you, through both your words and actions, about the person of Christ.

In an electronic age, in which people want involvement in everything from their television shows to their college life, a voice in everything from their parish to their work life, a book is a rather one-way method of talking. Seminars, small-group discussions, workshops, and other methods are preferable to book treatment. To offset the lack of participation, I must depend upon you, the reader, to make the best possible use of *Programs For Parish Councils* by adapting the material to your needs.

Books are often treated too well. This book, which is essentially a workbook, is meant to be roughed up, marked up, chewed, and parts of it spat out like pieces of hard-to-digest meat. A copy of this book in the hands of every one of your parish council's committee members will not guarantee either action or success. A rapid reading of the book, a gain in motivation and insight, and a liberal use of adaptation and discussion *will* guarantee success—with the grace of God and your own leadership efforts.

Is getting action the main complaint in your parish council? It's the nearly universal complaint in most parish councils. Why do you think this is so? If you are *not* getting action in your parish council, write below what you think are the reasons for this inactivity:

THE USE OF THIS BOOK

Discuss your thinking above with at least two, and preferably more, of your parish council members. This might be done by calling a meeting in your home; or, better, ask someone else to host the meeting in their home. The meeting should be brief, with a definite time limit, and a minimum of fuss made over arrangements. Coffee and cookies might be served. It might also be possible to have this discussion by devoting the first section of a regularly scheduled parish council board meeting to the topic.

After the discussion, write below all the reasons given to you by other persons for inaction in your parish council and add other facts and ideas that have occurred to you since you filled out the section above:

How do the two sections compare? Were there many similar complaints? Which ones do you agree with and which do you disagree with? Why? Can the list be divided into two parts, one representing items that can be taken care of through council board actions and the other showing items that require long-range planning and work? Discuss these items with council board members, if they were not already involved in the discussion. What are you asking them to do? What can other members of your discussion group do? What can you do? Is a follow-up meeting required? Why?

If you followed the suggestions above, you have already experienced the method of this book. Think about what happened. Reflection on this experience and the others that will be recommended will show you how to get action. Let's examine the process of your experience.

You were involved. You were not told; you were asked, "Is getting action the main complaint in your parish council?" You were asked what you knew about the problem. (Here the weakness of the book approach becomes clear, for if you did not see this as a problem, you can not tell me this, and the discussion continues only from my side. Still, if this difficulty is true in your case, it will at least serve for illustration purposes in our discussion on how to get action.)

You were involved with a problem. More important, that problem is one which is meaningful to you; it involves your self-interest, it is one about which you can do something, and you have a chance of success in your efforts. In other words, action can come if you see your self-interest involved, the problem is immediate, and you think that you can have some chance of success in tackling all or part of it.

(Suppose, however, that you are not now a member of a parish council. One of these elements, at least, is missing. You might see your self-interest involved in terms of thinking about the start of a parish council and in feeling that getting action will be a problem in your parish. You would not see the problem as something you could do something about at this time. The element of immediacy would be missing. You have probably, then, read to here without doing the discussions suggested above—unless you adapted the material to a discussion on how to get action *when* a council is organized in your parish. Such a discussion would probably end on a weak note, without any follow-through, how-

THE USE OF THIS BOOK

ever, because the persons you would talk with could not feel an immediate need for the problem or problems you would be bringing to their attention.)

You were involved with other persons. You were asked to talk with other people. In today's complex society, with a multiplicity of communities and increasing bonds of interdependence, there are few actions that can be either completed by one person or done without the approval and support of other persons. Even a dictator is limited in the things he can do without at least the tacit approval of public opinion.

Have you noticed another principle for getting action that we used here? We used an inductive rather than a deductive approach. This is the "see, judge, act" method used by the specialized movements (e.g., Christian Family Movement, Young Christian Students.) Based upon sound psychology and the experiences of the late Joseph Cardinal Cardijn, the founder of the Young Christian Workers, the see-judge-act approach starts with the facts of experience—starts "where you are"—rather than with moral, spiritual, and social principles. Through observation, through involvement with others, and through reflection the person discovers or experiences the principles which form his conscience and make up the matter of his judgment on when and how he acts.

These, then, will be the themes of this book—involvement with persons, preferably through personal contact and in small groups; starting with the facts; tackling problems which involve the self-interest of the group, which are immediate, and which promise to have in them some elements of success.

Out of these themes grow two principles which should be valid for the work of every parish council and the work of the Church generally:

1. Friendship and love must be the starting points

for any action if it is to provide for the growth of persons rather than the mere building of structures;

2. Friendship with Christ comes through the gifts of the Holy Spirit and through the friends of Christ. The Church might be described as the family of the friends of Christ. The parish council should be a way of making that family visible in a worshipping community that reaches out to the other communities where men live, work, and play.

Where, you might ask at this point, did all this about friendship come from, and then this friendship with Christ?

Perhaps the opening of this foreword did not sound very "spiritual," but take another look. Can you sit down with one person or a small group of persons, learn enough about them to know their needs and wants, and not become their friend? This does not mean that you cannot disagree with them or find something about their life pattern that you dislike. And if this friendship grows, can you say, as a Christian, that your concern will not grow to that ultimate concern—their redemption and eternal friendship with your own friend, Christ?

This concept can be realized by everyone. It can be worked out in the details of daily life and in the dynamics of committee work. If you and your parish council are worried about getting action that insures the growth of persons and their growth in friendship with Christ, this goal must become clearer and be articulated more fully in the words and actions of the council.

One use of *Programs For Parish Councils* would be for a parish council's board members and committee leaders to discuss the first four chapters of the book in a series of meetings. Use any or all of the discussion questions and resources at the end of each of these chapters in whatever way promotes the richest dialogue.

THE USE OF THIS BOOK

This will give you and the council leadership the development and the background for the work of adapting and leading the meetings outlined in the remaining chapters.

BERNARD LYONS

1. The Worshipping Community

> But because it is impossible for the bishop always and everywhere to preside over the whole flock in his Church, he cannot do other than establish lesser groupings of the faithful. Among these, parishes set up locally under a pastor who takes the place of the bishop are the most important: for in a certain way they represent the visible Church as it is established throughout the world.
>
> Therefore the liturgical life of the parish and its relationship to the bishop must be fostered in the thinking and practice of both laity and clergy; efforts also must be made to encourage a sense of community within the parish, above all in the common celebration of the Sunday Mass.
>
> CONSTITUTION ON THE SACRED LITURGY, ART. 42

MANY people have mixed emotions about their parish today. What are your feelings about your parish? Is it different than the one of your youth? How is it different?

Most of us have fond memories of the parish where we grew up. We remember it as dominated by the central figure of the pastor. We took our primary education in its school. The major junctures of our lives, and those of our families and friends, were marked in the baptisms, first communions, graduations, weddings, first Masses, and funerals in the parish church. The parish socials were the families' recreations, the young people's dating bureaus, and the older people's entertainment. Our right to be Americans—before John F. Kennedy was elected president—was spelled out in the ethnic names listed on the memorial plaque in the church commemorating those who had given their lives in service to their country. But we know that we can never return to the parish of our youth.

The crisis of the parish is not that the well-built structures and institutions did not serve their purposes. They served them well. The crisis is caused by the fact that the parishes and the Church did not change with the times. They were not flexible enough to match the growth of the persons who become self-confident within the parish ghetto. The parish did not change with the shifting needs and responsibilities of parishioners who became full-fledged members of a pluralistic society, undergoing its revolutions of rising aspirations, the constant massaging of its electronic media, and the painful curbing of its national sovereignty in a world shrinking through a growing interdependence and the threat of nuclear war.

If communications-theorist Marshall McLuhan is right, we live not in twentieth-century America, but in Bonanza Land. We not only see in St. Paul's mirror darkly, but we have that mirror aimed over our shoulder to where we have been. As a result we look at yesterday's patterns to determine today's problems and thus define how we shall live tomorrow. In this rear-view mirror we see the parish of our youth, which, if it was not rural, was at least small-town, even though it might have been part of a growing metropolitan area.

We admit some of the changes that make up the

problem we call the parochial crisis. We see the good that the parish did in the "Americanization" of our grandparents. The mistake comes in thinking that if only we can find needs the parish can fulfill to replace no-longer-existing needs, then we can have our old parish back with just a few changes. Some imagine that if we find new, unmet needs we can attract back many of the laymen who have "leaked" from the Church, inspire anew the priests who are searching for a role, and once again fill our churches and our parish halls.

Let us be more specific. An often-asked question is, who has the final authority in a school problem: the pastor, the parish council, or the school board? Better questions for a worshipping community to start with might be, Is there a school problem? What function does the school play in our worshipping community? Should there, in fact, be a school? Are there more effective programs we could undertake if there weren't a school? Are we putting too much time, energy, and money into an effort that duplicates the work of other communities and serves only a small percentage of our community? These are all legitimate questions for a community that must redefine itself in a shifting Church and world.

What we're dealing with here is not the theoretical problem of portraying the ideal parish or of creating an abstract parish that would seem to fit today's needs. We're dealing with the more pragmatic question of trying to define "worshipping community" for persons caught in the irony of living today while trying to shove yesterday's problems and patterns into a proper framework for tomorrow.

It is difficult to begin with the more basic question of whether there should be a school, when the school is there and has a staff ready to open the doors tomorrow morning for the children waiting outside. Still, unless we are free to consider the question of whether there should be a school, that rear-view mirror image is going to suggest strongly the kinds of problems and concerns that the worshipping community tries to tackle through its parish council.

What all this suggests is that the essential crisis today is a crisis in community. In this connection, two facts need to be stressed in any discussion of the present development of the parish.

The first fact is that the universal Church in its growing self-awareness, especially as expressed in Vatican Council II and in the ferment, dialogue, and polarization since, is coming to see itself as a community that must be decentralized. The growth of parish councils, the formation of priests' groups, the organizing of national conferences of bishops, as well as the continuing debate on such supposedly closed topics as priestly celibacy and contraception are a few of the evidences of this trend.

The second fact is that the Church, as this decentralizing community, is set among a growing multiplicity of communities. This is the fact acknowledged by such terms as the "socialization" used by Pope John XXIII, the "global village" proposed by Marshall McLuhan, and "the growing unity of all mankind not only in the blood, but in the spirit," envisioned by Teilhard de Chardin. The implication of this fact for the parish is that it can be best defined as a worshipping community and as a "service unit" of the local Church, joined in unity with the universal Church through the local bishop and the synod of bishops, headed by the pope.

Let us take a closer look at the twin trends of a decentralizing Church and proliferating communities.

If Figure 1 on page 5 is not a familiar one to you, at least the concept behind it is immediately recognizable.

THE WORSHIPPING COMMUNITY

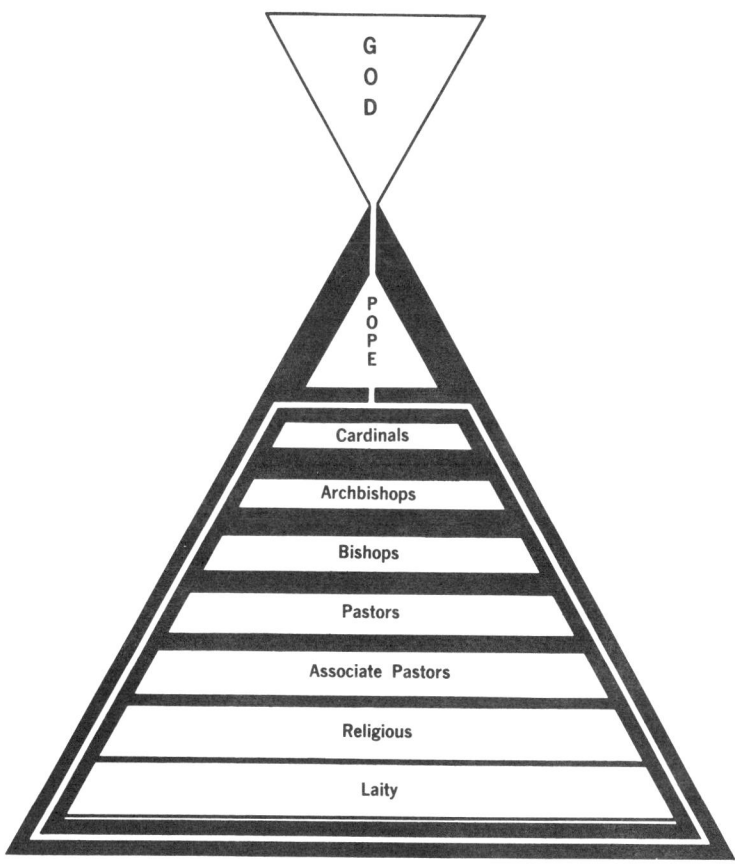

FIGURE 1

It is a concept that grew in the Church since the days of Constantine. Though many popes and bishops (notably St. Augustine and Pope St. Gregory VII) stressed an authority of service in the Christian community, the strongest, long-term image of the Church has been that represented by Figure 1. The clear outlines of this image may be seen in the Vatican I definition of papal infallibility and in the shift of the argument from the morality of contraception to the force of authority in Pope Paul VI's encyclical *On Human Life*.

There are many difficulties with such a concept of the Church, especially in relation to the idea of the Church as a community. Note in the figure that God is above the triangle or pyramid. We get a picture of an authoritarian God whose power is exercised by a single man, the pope. What does this do to the concept of the Incarnation? God became man. He came among us. His authority was so marked by the ideal of service that he refused to be crowned king.

The same figure that suggests a God above us, who is reached through a military-like chain of command, would seem to imply that the Holy Spirit is confined, like the pope, to the Vatican. Also, it would indicate that the gifts of the Holy Spirit are somehow circumscribed, so that, though they may be freely given, they can not be truly effective unless they operate within the proper chain of command.

Another difficulty with the concept of the Church expressed in Figure 1 is the dichotomy it implies, one destructive of the whole meaning of community, between those who govern and those who are governed. If authority is both a gift of the community and a service to it, a monarchical expression of that authority is a contradiction.

Now look at Figure 2. You may find it less orderly

THE WORSHIPPING COMMUNITY

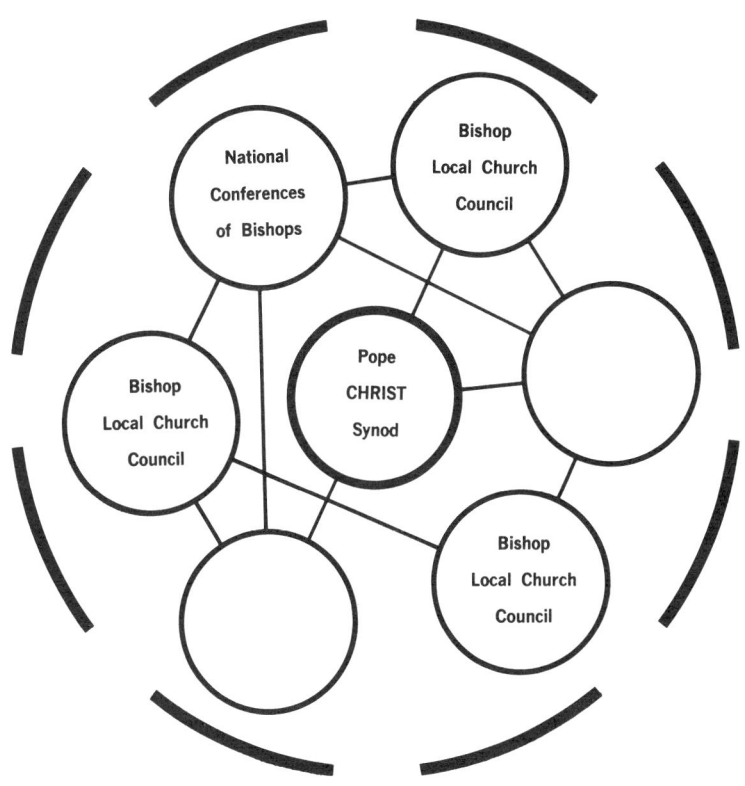

FIGURE 2

than Figure 1. Perhaps it gives you a sense of uneasiness and a feeling of ambiguity. Do not judge too hastily, however. Think out the implications of the concept behind the figure.

Note that Christ is in the center of the open circle. The fact of the Incarnation is thus given expression. The open circle suggests that people are drawn to Christ in a free society. They are free to come. None are excluded. They are free to leave, just as many left him when he promised to give them his body and blood to eat and drink.

This open circle of community suggests that authority is a gift to the entire community. The Holy Spirit operates through the community. The actions of that authority are expressed not only through the pope, but also through parish councils, diocesan councils, national councils, and through such groupings as national conferences, international conferences, and the synod of bishops.

Any person, whether cleric or layman, who is a member of this community thinks in terms of "we"—"we are the Church." The command was given to the Apostles to "feed my flock." It was a command given not to hirelings, but to members of the flock itself, for the Church is the flock and is not a kind of super-organization above and apart from it.

The picture of the Church outlined in Figure 2 is similar to the one described by Bernard Cardinal Alfrink at a meeting in the Netherlands in 1967 of the bishops from nineteen European countries.

At that meeting, Cardinal Alfrink said that Vatican Council II had given a renewed appreciation of the local Church, meaning the diocese. "That is, the Council has, in principle, put an end to the widespread custom of seeing and experiencing the local Church first of all and one-sidedly as merely a part of the one Catholic community of faith which is spread over the whole world and centrally governed by the successors of Peter. It has thereby broken through the tendency to accentuate the 'part-character' of the local Church above all else and, accordingly, to ascribe to the so-called 'world-Church' a one-sided, exaggerated significance at the expense of the innate, fundamental significance of the local Churches."

Cardinal Alfrink stressed that "it is in the local Churches that the one mystery of the Church of Christ is incarnated in a concrete way in our history. Without the reality of the local Churches [dioceses] the one Church of Christ is not to be found on earth." He then cited Vatican II documents to the effect that "bishops fulfill a special role in this local actualization of the whole mystery of the Church" because they receive the fullness of the sacrament of orders. He also gave a number of scriptural references to show that the thought and speech of the New Testament writers deliberately identified each local gathering of the faithful with the term "Church."

Cardinal Alfrink described the concept represented by Figure 2 optimistically: "The Council was certainly conscious of the tensions which such a variety . . . might effect with respect to the unity willed by Christ. But stronger than the fear and mistrust, which threaten to give no room to life, was the respectful conviction that both the living being of the Church and her catholicity would be served by this unavoidable multiformity. . . . Thus the variety of the local Churches forms the one world-embracing mosaic which in its whole brings the riches of Christ to fuller revelation than each separate stone, however precious this latter may be in itself. And in such a multiform unity the richness of human experience also comes to the fullest unfolding."

The Church is fully Church, then, at the diocesan level. It is here that we have the actualization of the whole mystery of the Church because of the fullness of orders. It follows that the parish is not, as it is often romantically described, "the mystical Body of Christ in miniature," nor is it fully Church. It can best be described as a specific kind of community. Many people call it a "worshipping community." This gives it a name that perhaps best describes its purpose and function.

One priest who criticized my last book, *Parish Councils*, made the point that I had not covered the theology of the parish. Of course I hadn't, for I don't believe there is such a thing. The parish is simply a pragmatic way of handling a large diocese. The bishop is the first pastor of the parish.

To disagree with this priest's position, which could be called the conservative or traditional one, is just as easy as to disagree with what might be labelled the liberal position. The latter seems to call for the creation of smaller parishes and the development of something that is loosely called "community," without a specifying adjective. As "parish" or "worshipping community" are used in this book, the terms apply equally to the standard boundary-defined parish, to the special "apostolate" to a university campus, hospital, or other special institution, or to the newer "floating parishes" or "experimental communities."

In the future the need will surely be for larger parishes and smaller dioceses. Both the Gospel and present-day social trends seem to call for this. On the one hand how can a bishop be a true pastor to two, three, or four hundred parishes? On the other hand, given the shortage of priests and the possibilities of the married diaconate, the problems of financing, organizing, and administration would seem better handled in large parishes. The parishes would not need the present large physical plants, but they would need a large population for support and flexibility, while operating more often than now through smaller groupings within the worshipping community.

Both the so-called liberal and conservative positions require the older pattern of the parish and the concept of the Church represented in Figure 1. The conservative seems to ignore the fact that the Church is decentralizing, while the liberal seems to push for a decentralized Church. The conservative wants to resist change and insists that the old lines of authority given in Figure 1 are still valid. The liberal welcomes changes in the Church, but wants them handed down authoritatively so that the conservatives will be forced to accept them.

Not only the decentralization of the Church, and new insights into the diocese as the local Church, call for the parish (whether with boundaries or not) to define itself more specifically as a worshipping community; the entire trend of proliferating communities in an age of mobility, freedom, electronic communication, and rapid travel leads to this development. In a global village where man has more possibilities than ever before to interact with his fellowmen and to form communities to express that interaction, communities become more single-purposed and specialized.

The parish that does not recognize the uniqueness of its interactions and does not relate to the other developing, specialized communities around it runs the risk of irrelevance. It will not have a vital role in the Church, and it will not have its necessary impact on those other communities.

The parish as worshipping community must celebrate those persons and good things around it and call attention to the need for reconciliation among persons and communities. Through that fullest expression of community that Christ gives us in giving himself to us in Communion, the worshipping community gives us a pattern to follow in all the communities of men.

DISCUSSION QUESTIONS

What do you believe has been the single most important change in parish life in your experience? Why?
Why do your fellow parishioners continue to attend the parish church? What needs are met for them in your parish? What do they like about their parish? What do they dislike about it?
Do you know persons who no longer go to your parish church? Why do they no longer go?
What is your definition of Church? Do you think of your parish as a "worshipping community"? How else might you define it?
Do you find the contrast between Figures 1 and 2 adequate to express the changes in the Church? In what ways do you agree? In what ways do you disagree?
Are you familiar with the term "socialization" as used by Pope John XXIII? What does the term mean to you?
Do you feel that Marshall McLuhan's term "global village" matches your experience of our changing world? List characteristics of this "global village" as they affect your everyday life.
Have you read any of the works of Teilhard de Chardin? Do you know anything about his life? Do you agree with the quotation given here about the growing unity of men? Do you, instead, see a great disharmony among men? Which is most noticeable in your parish? How would you define unity? Is such a unity possible in your parish?

RESOURCES

Arensberg, Conrad M., and Kimball, Solon T. *Culture and Community*. New York: Harcourt, Brace and World, Inc., 1965.

Blochlinger, Alex. *The Modern Parish Community*. New York: P. J. Kenedy and Sons, 1965.

Bordelon, Marvin, ed. *The Parish In A Time of Change*. Notre Dame, Ind.: Fides Publishers, 1967.

De Lubac, Henri, S.J. *Teilhard de Chardin, The Man and His Meaning*. New York: Hawthorn Books, 1965.

Greeley, Andrew M. *The Crucible of Change, The Social Dynamics of Pastoral Practice*. New York City: Sheed and Ward, 1968.

Gremillion, Joseph. *The Other Dialogue*. Garden City: Doubleday, 1965. (See especially the early chapters on socialization.)

Kopp, Sister Mary Audrey, SNJM. *The New Nuns: Collegial Christians*. Chicago: Argus Communications, 1968.

Lyons, Bernard. *Parish Councils: Renewing The Christian Community*. Techny, Ill.: Divine Word Publications, 1967. (See especially chapters on Crisis, Community, Leadership, and Unity.)

McCudden, John, ed. *The Parish In Crisis*. Techny, Ill.: Divine Word Publications, 1967.

McLuhan, Marshall. *Understanding Media: The Extensions of Man*. New York: McGraw-Hill, 1965.

———, and Fiore, Quentin. *The Medium is the Massage*. New York: Random House, 1967.

Murray, Michael H. *The Thought of Teilhard de Chardin: An Introduction*. New York: The Seabury Press, 1966.

Powell, John, S.J. *The Mystery of the Church*. Milwaukee: Bruce Publishing Co., 1967.

Smulders, Piet, *The Design of Teilhard de Chardin*. Glen Rock, N.J.: Newman Press, 1967.

Stern, Gerald E., ed. *McLuhan: Hot and Cool*. New York: The Dial Press, 1967.

Talec, Pierre, *Christian Presence in the Neighborhood*. Glen Rock, N.J.: Newman Press, 1967.

2. Christian Formation

> Nevertheless the liturgy is the summit toward which the activity of the Church is directed; at the same time it is the fountain from which all her power flows. For the goal of apostolic works is that all who are made sons of God by faith and baptism should come together to praise God in the midst of His Church, to take part in her sacrifice, and to eat the Lord's supper.
>
> The liturgy in its turn inspires the faithful to become "of one heart in love" when they have tasted to their full of the paschal mysteries; it prays that "they may grasp by deed what they hold in creed." The renewal in the Eucharist of the covenant between the Lord and man draws the faithful into the compelling love of Christ and sets them afire. From the liturgy, therefore, and especially from the Eucharist, as from a fountain, grace is channeled into us; and the sanctification of men in Christ and the glorification of God, to which all other activities of the Church are directed as toward their goal, are most powerfully achieved.
>
> CONSTITUTION ON THE SACRED LITURGY, ART. 10

"WHO do you say that I am?" If Christ asked you that question, how would you answer? It is important that we do answer. Most of us who were baptized as infants have not really faced up to the question. As a result we became "cultural Christians." We grew up in a family and environment that displayed certain patterns of Christianity, but we did not learn how to be critical of patterns that were contrary to the life of Christ.

This "clubhouse" Christianity made it difficult for us to see Christ in other persons, especially in those who were members of other denominations or perhaps of no denomination at all. Yet Christ is a personal choice of many persons who are not formal members of the Catholic Church. Christ created a revolution among persons. All of society is different today because of his entry as God-man into human history. It is impossible today to separate Christ and his message from the flow of history.

Do we have today a better view of and insight into human dignity than before Christ's time? Judged against the history of the Indians and the blacks in the United States, the terrible purges in Russia, and the attempted genocide in Hitler's Germany, we are tempted to answer the question negatively. But an overall view of man's development—including what he is ashamed of in his past—would show the growth of the idea of human dignity. Our American constitution is a benchmark in the articulation of this concept. Many of the documents of Vatican Council II develop the idea further. In many instances in history the concept of human dignity has not been stated in Christ-centered or in religious terms, but the working out of the concept, its articulation, came from the fulfillment of the life of the God-man in our history.

It is not adequate to answer Christ's "Who do you say that I am?" with a mere historical or biographical account. We can answer the question in this way for

Washington, Lincoln, John F. Kennedy, or Dr. Martin Luther King, Jr. But when we answer the question about Christ in an historical way we have only begun to scratch the surface.

Implicit in the question, "Who do you say that I am?" is a crucial question about ourselves: "Who am I?" Other historical figures had an effect upon us limited to history and our own acceptance of their values. But Christ, with his claim to be who he is, has affected us not only historically, but in the very essence of our humanity and for eternity—or else he is the biggest fraud in history. Another dimension was given to Christ's identity because he founded a Church. He claimed he had to return to the Father, otherwise the Holy Spirit would not come. But then he gave us His body to eat and his blood to drink.

In all of the seeming contradictions, the mysteries, the half-glimpsed truths here, it is certain that Christ is both the founder and the content itself of the Church. The problem for those who would follow Christ, who would be Christian, can not be answered simply by joining the Church, as if this act were little different than joining a club or some other organization. The problem for the Christian is to learn of Christ, to know Christ, to experience Christ so that he, the Christian, may be formed in Christ, put on Christ, grow in Christ.

The fullness of Christ can not be contained in any single program. Nor is it the result of education, of formal schooling. Formation in Christ requires a dynamic process like life itself. Only death stops the process or the need for it. There are, however, certain tested ways that men can use to put on Christ.

The Church founded by Christ is, of course, the principal source of knowledge and provides the best means of putting on Christ. Certainly the chief reason for the existence of the Church—worship and the eucharist—is the cornerstone to the process. There is more. Listen to the word of God. Reflect. Pray, both in word and in work. There is also an often overlooked way that persons put on Christ, that we can learn from Christ himself. This special way of putting on Christ can be seen in the way that he walked and talked among his friends, the Apostles and the disciples.

It would be well to read the Gospels with this one idea in mind—to see how Christ formed the Apostles. See how Christ was with them, not so much in a teacher-pupil relationship, but as a sharer in their lives. Notice how many of his lessons are formed around short, concrete examples, called parables. Many of his lessons were phrased in questions. He addressed large crowds, but spent most of his time with his small group of followers. He became their friend. He could feel the joy of a wedding celebration and weep over the death of a friend. His development of the Apostles often took the form of asking them to do him a favor. His closeness to them allowed him to use the most casual comments or unexpected pleas for help to teach a lesson.

Reflection on Christ and the way he walked, talked, and worked among us should also influence the way a parish council is formed and the way a committee system is organized. In a large parish it is easy to be distracted from the tasks of a worshipping community. A large physical plant and the demands of administration can lead us to place a priority on superficial contact through bulletin announcements, pulpit reminders, envelopes, and other devices. The mechanics become the goal. Persons become secondary or are ignored. One might answer that he cannot concentrate on a few persons, if as pastor, priest, deacon, or council officer, he must respond to all. Yet, can he not learn from Christ? Christ came to redeem the whole world, but worked closely with only a small number of persons.

Christ was a revolutionary. But he was a particular type of revolutionary. His revolution involved persons. He came for persons, with a nonviolent message about the coming of the kingdom of God. He didn't find it necessary to go to Rome, the seat of power, and destroy the Roman Senate. He was more interested in changing persons. He blew up ideas, not things. He broke the bonds of the imagination, not physical bonds. He knew that structures would change as persons developed in him. He further knew that persons formed in him would multiply himself, as they did his task of forming still others.

In a world concerned with power and authority Christ realized the subtle dangers inherent in the totalitarian approach that many otherwise good persons use when they wish to do so much *for* others. What Christ stressed were persons, decentralization, community, and freedom. The development of persons is aided, his life shows us, when we become sharers of their situations and work *with* them to achieve freedom and growth.

DISCUSSION QUESTIONS

Do you have a Bible or New Testament in your home? Do you have a life of Christ? How often do you read in these books? Do you enjoy reading them? If you don't enjoy reading them or do so infrequently, why do you think this is so?

What does the term "Christian formation" mean to you? What other words might better describe this concept for you?

What was Christ's essential message? Where, if anywhere, in the Gospels is it stated concisely?

How did Christ teach? What example of his teaching stands out most vividly in your mind? Why?

Would you describe Christ as a revolutionary? Why or why not?
How did you come to know Christ? List the ways.
Do the people with whom you come in contact each day know about Christ? What opportunities do they have to know about Christ?
Do you ever discuss Christ with your family? What about your relatives and friends? Do you ever talk about Christ with neighbors, co-workers, casual acquaintances? Why or why not?
Is there a pattern evident in your answers immediately above? Are you more likely to talk about Christ with relatives and friends than with others? Why?

RESOURCES

Betz, Otto. *What Do We Know About Jesus?* Philadelphia: Westminister Press, 1968.
Daniel-Rops, Henri. *Jesus and His Times.* Two volumes. Garden City: Image Books, 1954.
Gleason, Robert W., S.J. *Christ and the Christian.* New York: Sheed and Ward, 1959.
Jones, Alexander, ed. *The New Testament of the Jerusalem Bible.* Garden City: Doubleday, 1967.
Lepp, Ignace. *The Ways of Friendship.* New York: Macmillan, 1966.
Maloney, George A., S.J., *The Cosmic Christ, from Paul to Teilhard.* New York: Sheed and Ward, 1968.
Moore, Dom Sebastian. *No Exit.* Glen Rock, N.J.: Newman Press, 1968.
Rohrbach, Peter-Thomas, O.C.D. *Conversation With Christ.* Notre Dame, Ind.: Fides Publishers, 1956.
Sallaway, George H. *Follow Me: Be Human.* Baltimore: Helicon, 1966.
Schillebeeckx, Edward, O.P. *The Eucharist.* New York: Sheed and Ward, 1968.

3. The Parish Council

> The laity should accustom themselves to working in the parish in close union with their priests, bringing to the church community their own and the world's problems as well as questions concerning human salvation, all of which should be examined and resolved by common deliberation. As far as possible, the laity ought to collaborate energetically in every apostolic and missionary undertaking sponsored by their local parish.
>
> They should constantly foster a feeling for their own diocese, of which the parish is a kind of cell, and be ever ready at their bishop's invitation to participate in diocesan projects. Indeed, if the needs of cities and rural areas are to be met, laymen should not limit their cooperation to the parochial or diocesan boundaries but strive to extend it to interparochial, interdiocesan, national, and international fields. . . .
>
> DECREE ON THE APOSTOLATE OF THE LAITY, ART. 10

THE definition of the Church as an "open circle," said the late Archbishop Paul J. Hallinan of Atlanta, "is a correction—a rediscovery of the Gospels—what God wants his Church to be. In other times, other shapes may have been effective, but in a world grown used to self-reliance, dialogue, involvement, and the democratic way of life the pyramid just will not do. The 'open circle' is scripturally authentic and historically appropriate."

The open circle must characterize the collegial community at the parish level, too. Two quotes from Vatican Council II documents help us to define the Church and the parish council as an open circle.

In the Decree on the Apostolate of the Laity (Article 26), the bishops saw the Church not only as one open circle, but as a series of open circles:

"In dioceses, as far as possible, there should be councils which assist the apostolic work of the Church either in the field of making the gospel known and men holy, or in the charitable, social, or other spheres. To this end, clergy and religious should appropriately cooperate with the laity. While preserving the proper character and autonomy of each organization, these councils will be able to promote the mutual coordination of various lay associations and enterprises.

"Councils of this type should be established as far as possible also on the parochial, interparochial and interdiocesan level as well as in the national or international sphere."

The openness of the circle is stressed with the insight of the Gospel that the mission of the Christian community is not limited to itself but goes out to the whole world. In the Constitution on the Church the bishops said: (Article 9):

"So it is that this messianic people, although it does not actually include all men and may more than once look like a small flock, is nonetheless a lasting and sure seed of unity, hope, and salvation for the whole human race. Established by Christ as a fellowship of life, charity, and truth, it is also used by Him as an instrument for the redemption of all, and is sent forth into the whole

THE PARISH COUNCIL

world as the light of the world and the salt of the earth."

The most readily accepted definition of the parish council sees it as a way for the layman to participate in the administration and goals of his parish. This says something about the pyramidal structure of the Church today and recognizes the growing trend in our society for the involvement of people in organizations that affect them. It doesn't say enough, however, about the Gospel concept of the Christian community.

The parish council is a structured way for priests, religious, and laity to participate as equals (though with different roles and varied gifts of the Holy Spirit) not only in the administration of the parish, but also in the teaching, sanctifying, and governing of the "people of God." (The phrase "people of God" includes everybody, not just the laity. Layman, pope, deacon, priest, nun, and brother may say "we" in talking about the Church.)

The parish council is the strong skeleton for the body of the liturgical community. It helps to give form, efficiency, and outline to that group of people who through their corporate worship and witness make the Church visible locally.

This definition of a parish council may apply not only to the traditional parish (i.e., one with boundaries, plant, school, etc.), but also to the parishes known as experimental communities in such areas as Oklahoma City-Tulsa, Madison, Wisconsin, and Atlanta, Georgia. You will recall that, in the view adopted here, the parish is simply a way of making that open circle of the local Church, or diocese, visible.

Many people would find this book more satisfying if I were more definite and provided a detailed schematic or organizational chart for a parish council. To do such a thing would be against the spirit of the way that Christ forms men into community. If you don't feel this yet, I ask that you review the points made earlier in this book, urge you to reflect upon them, and encourage you to patiently work in the style of Christ. An increased awareness and hope may come also from exploring the experiences of others. Visits to other parish councils and joint meetings with neighboring councils, including those of our other Christian brothers in the Protestant and Orthodox faiths, will be found helpful.

Your council board members may also find it helpful to read *Parish Councils: Renewing the Christian Community*. In that book there are several chapters that give concrete examples of parish councils, there is a model constitution, and an outline of a parish leadership course. Again, there is the warning, as with this book, that the material should be digested and adapted to and by the persons in your local community.

Now let us look at the open circle pictured in Figure 3. Again, there is a kind of disorder about it, but this is in the spirit of the Gospel and of democracy. Note that Christ is the center. The parish council and the pastor are in the center. The council, through representative elections, provides an authority of service, in the same way that the pastor does. In addition, the pastor, as the delegate of the bishop, the first pastor, provides a particular kind of unity with the local Church. (Further democracy will be expressed in this arrangement when, in the future, bishops are again elected by the whole local Church.)

Note, too, in Figure 3 that we have not shown an organizational ladder. Each organization (the unmarked circle can represent such organizations) and committee within the parish community enjoys its own autonomy. The center circle is open, showing that the worshipping community is a free society. The lines of authority and service to the organizations and committees reach out

THE PARISH COUNCIL

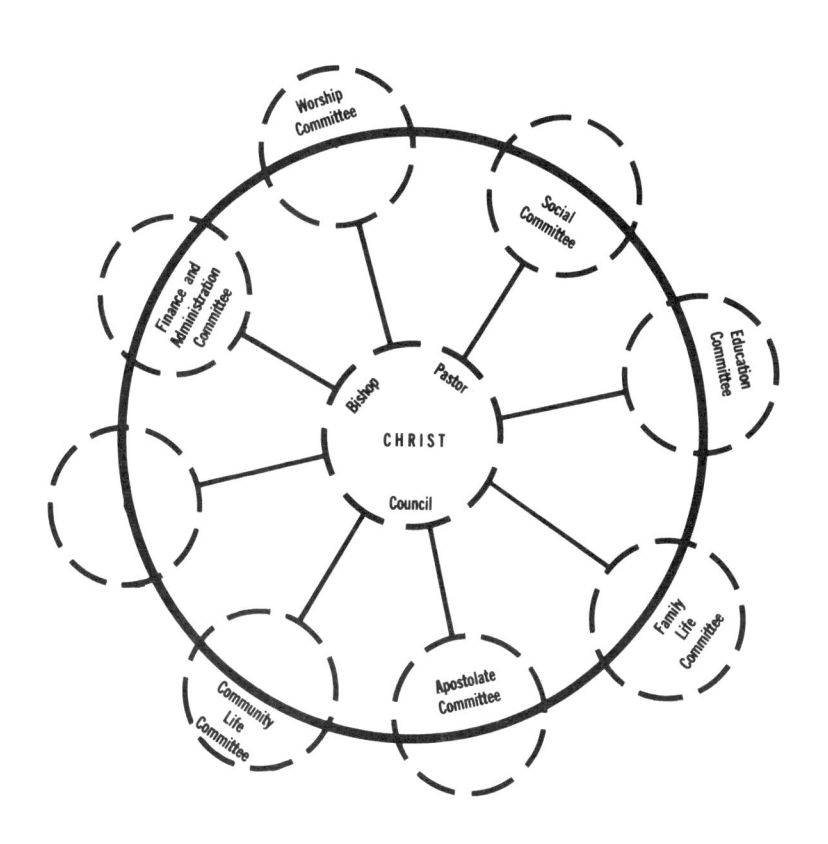

FIGURE 3

beyond the enclosed circle through the members of the groups who by baptism and participation in the Eucharist are definite members of the worshipping community, but who interact with and are members of many other communities. Members of the education committee reach out to many communities (local PTA's, adult-education groups, community school-boards) not shown in Figure 3. In the same way members of the community life committee reach out to such communities as block clubs, community organizations, League of Women Voters, and countless other groups.

All of the committees and the organizations (again represented by the untitled circle) may or may not be present in particular parishes, but where they are present they have their own autonomy. In addition, they have lines of service and communication among each other. The education committee will need to work with the finance and administration committee for particular budgets; the apostolic committee will need to cooperate with several of the other committees to put on successful information or inquiry classes; and so on. In certain cases, the total assembly may wish to reserve particular policies and decisions to itself so that committees will have to submit programs and projects to the council board or to the entire membership of the worshipping community.

The worshipping community expresses unity with the universal Church in an additional way, other than through the local pastor as delegate of the bishop. Many parish organizations have not only horizontal links of unity with other groupings within the local worshipping community, but also vertical links with diocesan-wide, national, and international organizations (e.g., diocesan CCD programs, national sodalities, and international groups such as the Christian Family Movement).

The unity of the parish council with the local Church

and the universal Church may be expressed by placing Figure 3, in your imagination, within Figure 2 (see page 7). The bishop is in the center, not for purposes of expressing authority alone, but more for indicating that as the first pastor he draws all men to Christ. This is the rationale for the existence of the open circle, for which he is the presiding officer.

Again, in this open circle of the local Church we find a rather haphazard arrangement of details. The emphasis should be on the development of persons and the necessary flexibility of this process, rather than on structures and chains of command. You might imagine within the circle of the local Church the open circles of other collegial forms, such as parish councils, interparish councils, the diocesan council, the senate of priests, and many other forms. All express unity rather than particular positions within a hierachy of authority in the diocese. The local Church, like the worshipping community, is a grouping of equals who share their varied gifts and ministries of service.

DISCUSSION QUESTIONS

Should the parish council be concerned with more than assisting the pastor in the finances and administration of the parish? Why or why not?

How is the parish council defined in this chapter? Do you agree or disagree? Why?

In your own words, how would you define the parish council?

Look at Figure 3. What does it tell you about the parish? Do you agree with this schematic approach?

Draw a graphic representation of the way your parish looks to you. Perhaps you could do one drawing showing the way your parish functions now, and another that would try to represent what an ideal worshipping community should contain and how it would function. Look at Figures 1 and 2, in Chapter 1. How do they relate to Figure 3 given in this chapter?

RESOURCES

Books and Booklets

Abbott, Walter M., S.J., ed. *The Documents of Vatican II, With Notes and Comments by Catholic, Protestant and Orthodox Authorities.* New York: Association Press and Guild Press, 1966.

Association of Chicago Priests (ACP). "Parish Councils," Report Prepared by the Priests' Committee on Parish Councils. Chicago: ACP, 1307 S. Wabash Ave. (60605), 1968.

Broderick, Robert C. *The Parish Council.* Chicago: Franciscan Herald Press, 1968. (Has sample charter, constitutions, leadership questionnaire.)

Congar, Yves, O.P. *Lay People in the Church.* Westminster, Md.: Newman Press, 1965.

Lyons, Bernard. *Parish Councils: Renewing the Christian Community.* Techny, Ill.: Divine Word Publications, 1967. (Why, how of parish councils, what some are doing now. Emphasis on freedom, cooperation. Nine chapters, including unity through local Church, training of council members. Appendices have suggested constitution, standing committees, selected readings.)

McCudden, John, ed. *The Parish in Crisis, Approaches to the Changing Urban Parish.* Techny, Ill.: Divine Word Publications, 1967.

National Council of Catholic Men, *Parish Councils: A Report on Principles, Purposes, Structures, and Goals.* Washington, D.C.: Parish Service Bureau, NCCM, 1967.

_____. *Sample Parish Council Constitutions* (part of Parish Council Package, $3). Washington, D.C.: Parish Service Bureau, NCCM, 1967.

O'Neill, David P. *The Sharing Community, Parish Councils and Their Meaning.* Dayton, Ohio: Pflaum Press, 1968.

Ryan, E. E., C.M.F. "Lay Participation in Parish Administration, A Step by Step Program for Setting Up Parish Councils." Thesis,

55 pp. ($1, author, Catholic Student Center, Box C.C., LSU, Baton Rouge, La. 70803), 1967.

St. Mary's Parish, "Sermons and Letters, in Preparation for Organizing a Council." $1 from St. Mary's Church, 303 N. 4th St., Oregon, Ill., 1967.

Selected Articles

Brown, William E. "The Hang-Up Over Structure," *America,* Oct. 19, 1968.

Byrne, Robert J. "Pastors and Laity Share Responsibility," with chart of eight parish charters, *St. Louis Review,* Feb. 10, 1967 (reprinted in June, 1967, *Catholic Digest*).

Gintoft, Ethel. "Can Parish Councils Really Work?" *St. Anthony Messenger,* March, 1968. (This is a special issue, "The Parish In a Time of Crisis," and has several related articles.)

Greeley, Andrew M. "The New Community," *The Critic,* June-July, 1966.

Lyons, Bernard, "How To Organize a Parish Council," *Act,* June, 1968.

_____. "Parish Councils: Creating Christian Partnerships," *Extension,* May, 1967.

_____, "Parish Councils in the Chicago Archdiocese," *The Chicago Voice,* Feb. 5, 1968.

"Laymen's Rights," editorial. *Western Catholic Reporter* (Edmonton, Alberta) Jan. 19, 1967.

Winter, Art, "Parish Councils Grow in U.S. Church," two-part series. *National Catholic Reporter,* June 21, 28, 1967.

Selected Aids

Filmstrips that can be adapted to parish council committees, including "All Doctrine Is Social Doctrine," "Race and The Christian," "Confirmation: The Sacrament of Witness," "Witness Only the Layman Can Give," and others: Thomas S. Klise Co., P.O. Box 3418, Peoria, Ill. 61614.

Parish Council. Monthly bulletin. James F. Colaianni, ed. $2 annually. The Liturgical Conference, 2900 Newton St., N.E., Washington, D.C. 20018.

Discussions, talks, group dynamic approaches to forming and stimulating parish councils. Write: Bernard Lyons, Suite 1612, 29 E. Madison, Chicago, Ill. 60602 (312) ST2-4741.

PROGRAMS FOR PARISH COUNCILS

"Parish Service Program," under direction of Michael Cook, designs and makes available guidelines and materials, including bulletin "Parish Today," which reports on trends, experiences, and plans for parish development. Annual fee: $25. Write: Parish Service Program, NCCM, 1312 Massachusetts Ave., N.W., Washington, D.C. 20005.

Redemptorists' Parish Analysis. Evaluation of parish attitudes; questionnaires concerning ecumenism, community, Church, etc., processed by computer. Write: Rev. Patrick B. Sullivan, C.SS.R., Liguori, Mo. 63057.

4. Council Committees

> Christ's redemptive work, while of itself directed toward the salvation of men, involves also the renewal of the whole temporal order. Hence the mission of the Church is not only to bring to men the message and grace of Christ, but also to penetrate and perfect the temporal sphere with the spirit of the gospel. In fulfilling this mission of the Church, the laity, therefore, exercise their apostolate both in the Church and in the world, in both the spiritual and the temporal orders. These realms, although distinct, are so connected in the one plan of God that He Himself intends in Christ to appropriate the whole universe into a new creation, initially here on earth, fully on the last day. In both orders, the layman, being simultaneously a believer and a citizen, should be constantly led by the same Christian conscience.
>
> DECREE ON THE APOSTOLATE OF THE LAITY, ART. 5

COMMITTEES have a bad name; a camel, it is said, is a horse designed by a committee. Yet the courageous and patient bearing of the frustrations often caused by committee work, can help us to keep in mind that the purpose of our parish council committees is the growth of persons in both human-ness and in Christ.

The mere achievement of particular projects and tasks should not be enough for the Christian. Action, of course, must be emphasized. Service to our fellowmen is a requirement of Christ, and one of the ways we are formed in Christ is through action—servicing the needs and wants of others.

It is not an easy task to keep a proper balance between action and escape into perpetual preparation of ourselves for action through endless reading and discussion. To put the problem in another way, life is not a matter of choosing either the liturgy or social action as the starting point in the formation of a person in Christ. Formation is a dynamic process. Eucharistic celebration and its pricking of our conscience about the need for reconciliation around us, should move us to the world and the world should move us back to the banquet table of Communion. And so on. There should be dynamic interaction between liturgy and social action. In the same way, committee work is interaction between dialogue and action, gathering in and going out, planning and evaluating, observing and reflecting, doing it ourselves and motivating others, thinking it and feeling it through, knowing definitely and flying by the seat of our pants.

American industrial organizations and various other kinds of groups in this country have developed committee work into a near-science through such approaches as group therapy and group dynamics. In the Catholic Church, we have only begun to feel the effects of these democratic forms, since our strongly authoritarian structure inhibited their earlier use. The resources listed after this chapter will help in the discovery of the potential and the techniques of group work for those not already familiar with them. Here we wish to deal with the specific types of committees found in parish councils and to indicate something of their scope, especially for council board members, who will need a general view of the material covered in the next seven chapters.

It would be helpful to review Appendix B in *Parish Councils: Renewing the Christian Community* for a description and list of possible actions for the committees treated in this book. The list of the seven committees was made after a review of the typical committees that parish councils were establishing. The only change made in this previous list by our treatment here is the calling of the Liturgical Committee by the more understandable name of the Worship Committee.

There is no formula or easy way to tell which committee and how many committees a particular parish council should have. Time, experience, experimentation, the issues, and the personalities of your parish community will determine the type and number. The committees treated in this book seem to be most appropriate for the functioning of a worshipping community and are the ones most often found in parish councils.

There are other single-purpose committees (e.g., constitution and by-laws) and temporary committees (e.g., committee for the annual meeting of the parish council assembly) which we have not treated here. It would be impossible for one book to treat of all the possible committees. Also, the special purpose and temporary nature of the other committees usually dictate their meetings and little difficulty is experienced with them in terms of definition.

Most of the committees treated here are required by the nature of the worshipping community. A worship committee is obviously needed if true participation is to be achieved. A finance and administration committee is necessary, even if the particular worshipping community has no property or boundaries, as in the case of some of the experimental communities. There are still halls to be rented, living expenses for the priest, collections for diocesan programs, and provisions to be made for the poor and the missions. Education is absolutely necessary in any worshipping community, but it should not be restricted to concern about the parochial school alone. Special religious courses, inquiry classes, adult education programs, and other activities are needed if the role of teacher is to be more fully exercised by the bishop in your worshipping community. The apostolic, community life, social, and family life committees are appropriate to any worshipping community, though their titles and their definitions might differ from one community to another.

Many parish councils (possibly looking through that rear-view mirror) have a sports committee or youth committee. There may be special needs for these committees in some locations. I, however, do not favor such specialization in standing committees. If there is a need for sports activities in your community—and the need is most likely there—the need can probably be met in cooperation with other church, civic, and fraternal groups. As with the parochial school which absorbs so much of the energy, time, and finances of the typical parish, sports programs and other activities that preoccupy parishioners may duplicate activities that could be more efficiently handled by another agency, community, or by cooperation between several such groupings.

In regard to youth committees, I feel that they do not build up community. The youth committee is established to do things *for* youth. It seems preferable that young people should be involved in their own groups, such as the Young Christian Students, and that in the larger parish and civic community they should be equal members and voted to office and assigned tasks equal to their education, skills, and interests. There is no reason to treat children as mere subjects of adult institutions, nor do I feel that it contributes to preparing children for participation in the parish or in the larger social order to exclude them from that participation until a certain arbitrary age is reached.

On the other end of the age scale, there is little need for a senior citizens committee. Perhaps a senior citizens club or organization (whether within the parish, covering several parishes, or across denominational lines) might fulfill a need. In terms of the worshipping community, senior citizens, with their years of experience and their increased leisure hours, will be able to contribute greatly to all of the committees.

(Before going on, I'd like to comment that the generation gaps, on either end of the scale, are nearly as serious a problem in America as the racial gaps and denominational gaps. Segregation by age is divisive and against the concept of a community of equals. There is no need even to discuss the white racism and the prejudice against women in the Church. These attitudes are totally against what Christ taught us about human dignity. We can't ignore these sins in our society, and no parish council can succeed as a Christ-centered worshipping community if it ignores them within its open circle.)

In beginning to establish committees, it would be well to think through the committees outlined in the next seven chapters. Discussions throughout the community and in parish council board sessions will indicate other committees that might be formed. These might be of a special or of a temporary nature, or they might be made subcommittees of more comprehensive committees.

Some parishes have used a time and talent census to determine the interests of their parishioners and to enlist their active participation in committee work or in special projects. Such a device can be effectively used if it is accompanied by personal contact and follow-up to see that the person recruited has been given enough information and has begun to make progress in the assignment he has chosen.

The inserting of a form in the weekly bulletin is the least effective way to solicit the generous giving of time. (Why is it that only special fund-drives, often conducted by professionals, seem to require the concentrated training of leaders and door-to-door solicitation and personal contact?) The most effective way to build up committees is to have them formed around real issues and needs and to make the leadership of the committee responsible for recruiting, though other parishioners may refer interested persons to a particular committee. (For example, if the community life committee has a program of welcoming each new family to the community, they might help newcomers to get established in a committee or project. It certainly gives a much warmer reception than an introduction to a large gathering or the parish as a whole.) The committee itself should make as many of its meetings as possible available (all should be open) to the other members of the worshipping community, with convenient hours and accessible locations. This will inform the entire worshipping community of the committee's activities and gain active support for it.

Active recruiting for certain committees, especially at their founding, might be done among groups already a part of the parish. Certain persons in these established groupings will find the committee a continuation of their previous interests. For example: commentators, lectors, and choir members are often the most natural recruits for a worship committee. Ushers, leaders of men's clubs and altar societies, and persons with special training in management, finance, etc. are likely recruits for a finance and administration committee. Parents who have children in the school, educators, and those already active in varied fields of adult and specialized education (Gabriel Richard courses, credit unions, CCD) are most likely to express first interest in the education committee. Members of the Christian Family Movement, active workers for Cana Conferences, professional counselors, and persons from similar groups will want to contribute their time through the family life committee.

* * *

The meetings in the following chapters for seven different parish council committees are suggestions only. They should be adapted to your own needs and those of your particular worshipping community.

If you need further information on leading group discussions, you might review the resource list following Chapter Four.

To make the most effective use of these meetings, you must, above all, *adapt*. Read over the meetings that concern your committee. Drop, add to, and change meetings according to the way that you see it.

If you elect to follow the patterns of the meetings suggested here, reread each meeting before your group discussion. You will find more than enough discussion material in each meeting. Use what seems to be most pertinent to you. Don't hesitate to drop a topic when the group seems uninterested. Don't be afraid to cut off discussion at the height of interest.

Evaluation questions are contained in each set of meetings. For your own purposes, you can judge the progress of your committee from the answers to these questions and also to a constant review of the following: Are members doing the actions they agree to do? Is your committee growing? Are friendships being formed? Are members beginning to express concern over the development of the committee and the worshipping community and taking initiative in and out of the meetings? You will have to experiment to answer a number of questions. In the beginning, meetings should not run over two hours. They should probably be held in members' homes. Meetings should be scheduled no more frequently than every two weeks, and no less frequently than every four weeks.

DISCUSSION QUESTIONS

In your own words, what is the general purpose of parish council committees? Do they differ from committees found in industry or in civic groups? If so, how do they differ?

If you have a parish council, list the committees you now have. After each committee, list the needs it is fulfilling. Rate each committee on its effectiveness. Why are certain ones rated more effective than others? Are there any committees that are not functioning well? What seems to be the problem? Do you have committees that are duplicating the efforts of other groups in your area?

Do you think a parish council should have a committee on ecumenism? Why or why not? Is it possible that ecumenical activities might be promoted by several of the committees outlined in this book? Is it practical that the worship committee include members from other local congregations, promote lectures or discussions on forms of worship among several Churches? Can the community life committee establish contact and cooperate with the human-relations programs of the social concerns committee of the local Methodist Church? How does the education committee relate to the PTA of your local high school?

Should there be committees for youth and senior citizens? Why or why not?

COUNCIL COMMITTEES

Could a woman be elected president of your parish council? Should a woman be elected president of your parish council? Why or why not? How representative is the membership of your committees? Are there people under thirty active in the committees? Are senior citizens adequately represented? What about geographical representation, with persons from various areas of the parish? Are the men as active as the women? Do you have any non-Catholics in any of the committees?

RESOURCES

Arlin, Marshall. *The Dynamics of Group Discussion, A Guide to Effective Dialog.* Chicago: Argus Communications, 1968.

Baird, John E. *A Guide to Conducting Meetings.* Nashville: Abingdon Press, 1965.

Bennett, Thomas R., II. *The Leader and the Process of Change.* New York: Association Press, 1962.

Brightbill, Charles K. *The Challenge of Leisure* Englewood Cliffs, N.J.: Prentice-Hall, 1963.

Buchanan, Paul C. *The Leader and Individual Motivation.* New York: Association Press, 1962.

Cunningham, James V. *The Resurgent Neighborhood.* Notre Dame, Ind.: Fides Publishers, 1965.

Fulcher, Gordon S. *Common Sense Decision-Making.* Evanston, Ill.: Northwestern University Press, 1965.

Grumme, Marguerite. *Basic Principles of Parliamentary Law and Protocol.* Westwood, N.J.: Fleming H. Revell Co., 1953.

Hudnut, Robert K. *Surprised by God, What It Means To Be A Minister in Middle Class America Today.* New York: Association Press, 1967.

Lippit, Gordon L., and Seashore, Edith. *The Leader and Group Effectiveness.* New York: Association Press, 1962.

Luft, Joseph. *Group Processes, An Introduction to Group Dynamics.* Palo Alto, Calif.: The National Press, 1963.

McCormick, Sister Rose M., M.M. *The Global Mission of God's People.* Maryknoll, N.Y.: Maryknoll Publications, 1967.

Morgan, John S. *Practical Guide to Conference Leadership.* New York: McGraw-Hill, 1966.

Mulholland, John, and Gordon, George N. *The Magical Mind, Key to Successful Communication.* New York: Hastings House, 1967.

Oppenheimer, Martin, and Lakey, George. *A Manual For Direct Action.* Chicago: Quadrangle Books, 1964.

Pierson, Robert H. *So You Want To Be A Leader!.* Mountain View, Calif.: Pacific Press Publishing Assn., 1966.

Rahner, Karl, S.J. *Christian in the Market Place.* New York: Sheed and Ward, 1966.

Schaller, Lyle E. *Community Organization: Conflict and Reconciliation.* Nashville: Abingdon Press, 1966.

Seifert, Harvey. *Power Where The Action Is, Making Ethical Decisions in Your Job, in Your Community, in Politics.* Philadelphia: Westminster Press, 1968.

Stuber, Stanley I., and Nelson, Claud D. *Implementing Vatican II In Your Community.* New York: Association Press, 1967.

Thelen, Herbert A. *Dynamics of Groups at Work.* Chicago: University of Chicago Press, 1954.

Wagner, Russell H., and Arnold, Carroll C. *Handbook of Group Discussion.* Boston: Houghton Mifflin Co., 1965.

Weschler, Irving R. *The Leader and Creativity.* New York: Association Press, 1962.

Wilson, Robert L., and Davis, James H. *The Church in the Racially Changing Community.* Nashville: Abingdon Press, 1966.

5. Worship

> No one can come to me
> unless he is drawn by the Father who sent me,
> and I will raise him up at the last day.
> . . . .
> I tell you most solemnly,
> everybody who believes has eternal life.
> I am the bread of life.
> Your fathers ate the manna in the desert
> and they are dead;
> but this is the bread that comes down from heaven,
> so that a man may eat it and not die.
> I am the living bread which has come down from heaven.
> Anyone who eats this bread will live for ever;
> and the bread that I shall give
> is my flesh, for the life of the world.
>
> JOHN 6:44, 47-51

THE central action of the parish—the celebration of the Eucharist—must be the chief concern of the worship committee. This committee must find ways to bring true participation, beyond mere standing and singing, to the community's corporate worship. The committee must also see to it that the members of the community, through cooperation with other committees and persons, are prepared to celebrate the good things in their lives at the eucharistic banquet and are equipped to take Christ's peace everywhere that reconciliation is needed.

First Action Meeting

See

What is the Mass schedule in your parish?

How many people worship in your parish church each Sunday? How many persons worship in your church each weekday? How many persons are registered in your worshipping community?

Are there special Masses (e.g., children's Mass, guitar Mass) regularly held in your parish? Are home Masses celebrated in your parish?

Judge

Do you personally like the changes in the Mass that have been made since Vatican II? What specifically do you like? What do you dislike? What other changes, if any, would you like to see made?

How do other parishioners feel about the changes that were made? Can you recall any conversations or incidents that indicate the feeling of some of the parishioners? Relate them to the group.

Have you visited other parishes nearby or in other parts of the country? If so, how do their liturgical services compare with those in your parish? What changes have been made in these other parishes that are not in effect in your parish? What changes has your parish made that have apparently not been made in other churches you have visited?

How would you rate your parish—traditional, moderate, progressive, etc.—in terms of the liturgical services conducted there?

How do you think Christ would react to the worship services in your parish? What would he like? What would he dislike?

Act

Are any actions suggested by your discussions? If so, list them on the next page:

Can each member of the worship committee interview two persons on the liturgical changes in your parish since Vatican II? How aware are your fellow parishioners of the changes? Do they like the changes? Do they wish for a return to the older forms? What were their first reactions? (If at all possible, interviews should be made with persons representing a wide variety of opinions. If you know of persons who are active with Una Voce or other traditionalist groups, or persons who are active in experimental groups, be sure to include them. Include some persons under twenty-five years of age in the interviews, too.) Write your assignment here:

If you know of Catholics who do not attend Mass regularly or have not participated in Mass for some time, interview them. Are they aware of the changes? Have any of them found the new participation more attractive? Have others found it a handicap to a regular return to the Mass and sacraments?

In preparation for the next meeting: How many members does your committee have? Are the members representative of the parish in terms of differing viewpoints on the liturgy, geographical location, sex, age, racial and ethnic groups? Who would you recommend for membership?

Second Action Meeting

See

Have each member report on his actions since the last meeting. Discuss the interviews in detail. (Names of the interviewees should not be given without their permission. Where it would help to understand the remarks and attitudes some description of the interviewee might be given.)

Judge

Do you have a better picture now of the attitudes of your fellow parishioners towards the changes in the Mass since Vatican II? Do you feel the need for more information?

Did any of the people you interviewed indicate any need for further changes in the worship service? What were they, if any?

What does the term "worship" mean to you? Is it an obligation of every person? Or, an obligation only for Catholics?

What do you know about the history and development of the Mass? Discuss briefly.

Act

What action or actions might be suggested by your discussions? Write them here:

If you feel the need for more information on how your fellow parishioners think and feel about your parish worship services, what would you recommend as an effective and efficient way to get this information? Is it necessary to do a full census survey? Could a questionnaire be included in the weekly bulletin and the results reported back within a week or two? Could each member of your committee host an informal meeting at his home and lead a discussion on this topic? Could a lecture-discussion, led by someone from the parish or the diocesan liturgical commission, be held? Write your other ideas here:

Are home Masses now being offered in your parish? Why not? A good way to educate people about the Mass and give them a greater sense of community is to start a home-Mass program. A beginning might be made by having each member of the worship committee host a home Mass or arrange one home Mass. The discussion meeting suggested in the previous action above might be held following the Mass in each home. If you and/or the group decide on this action, write your brief plan below:

Where might you get more information about the Mass? Is there a diocesan liturgy commission? Ask the priests to recommend material. If you have a parish library or a reading rack in the back of church, is it possible to arrange that appropriate literature be displayed? What else might be done to promote knowledge and love of the Mass?

Third Action Meeting

See

Report on all actions taken since the last meeting. Discuss.

Have any home Masses been held or arranged since the last meeting? Discuss. Have any further interviews or discussions been held or arranged? Discuss.

How many commentators and lectors do you have in your parish? Are there sufficient men to fill the schedule in your parish? Are all the men who wish to participate as commentators and lectors included in the schedule? Are commentators and lectors available during the week?

Do the high school students and the younger men of the parish participate as commentators and lectors? If not, why not?

Are the commentators and lectors fairly representative of the parish? Does the schedule involve a good percentage of the men in the parish?

What sort of training did the commentators and lectors receive? What provisions are made for follow-up training? Are materials given to the men so that they might prepare the readings and comments in advance?

Judge

What is your evaluation of the job done by the commentators and lectors? Do they speak distinctly? Do they add to the fitting conduct and participation of the Mass? Can they be heard with ease by the entire congregation? Is the microphone system adequate in your parish?

Would women make good commentators and lectors? Should women be commentators and lectors? Why or why not?

WORSHIP

Act

Write below any action or actions suggested by your discussion:

How can you enlist more men in the parish as commentators and lectors? Is it possible to hold a meeting of the commentators and lectors and ask each man to get one new person in the program? Might a chairman be appointed and a special subcommittee created for this continuing project?

(Two stumbling blocks for many men in volunteering for these assignments is a shyness or reluctance to speak in public and their ignorance of the Mass. This can usually be overcome in a brief training program, conducted in one to three sessions. Enlist the support of the priests, an experienced commentator or two, and perhaps someone from the education committee. The sessions should be held in Church. Perhaps a "dry Mass" might be held, with a priest or layman going through the steps of the Mass without the consecration and communion. This will help new commentators and lectors to understand the Mass better, see it from the different perspective of the altar, and help them gain confidence in knowing when and where comments and readings are to be made. Many men, too, will need the practice of speaking with a microphone and a few of the other techniques of public speaking.)

If you discussed the possibility of women serving as commentators and lectors, is there any further research to be done; any action to be taken?

Fourth Action Meeting

See

Report and discuss all actions taken since the last meeting.

Have you tried arranging a number of home Masses or discussions on the Mass? Report any of those scheduled, and discuss the experiences of those that have been held.

Do you and your fellow parishioners generally know enough about the Mass? Give details, examples, and incidents that illustrate what you know about the Mass and what you do not know about it.

Judge

What seems to be the biggest need in regard to knowledge of and full participation in the Mass?

Would a program to involve all the parishioners in home Masses and discussions answer the need for preparation, knowledge, and full participation in the Mass? Why or why not?

Act

Write below the actions suggested by your discussions:

If you have decided on a program of home Masses, discuss the best ways to make the program effective. The following hints and questions may be of help.

Would it be more efficient to set up a permanent subcommittee to work with the priests and arrange the schedules for home Masses? Are there diocesan directives you should be aware of?

Is your parish now divided into areas? If not, is it possible for your subcommittee to make such divisions so that home Masses might be scheduled on a somewhat regular basis throughout various parts of the parish and thus be made accessible to most persons?

Would it be helpful to have an information sheet prepared and duplicated, to give to the hosts and hostesses to help them in preparations for the home Mass?

Can arrangements be made so that various persons might serve as co-hosts, including shut-ins, the chronically ill, and those living in small apartments or institutional settings where they would not have the opportunity to offer their home?

Are there prejudices towards and problems about home Masses that you should be aware of? Your previous interviews and the experiences of persons who hosted and attended home Masses in your parish would help in determining ways to overcome objections.

What are the best hours for home Masses? Do hosts and hostesses need help in inviting friends and neighbors to attend? Is it wise to serve refreshments after the home Mass? Should the host, the priest, or another guest lead a discussion following the Mass, or should it be more informal and a general discussion?

Experience and experimentation on a number of these points will be necessary. A subcommittee will be helpful in order to make the schedule, follow through on the details, evaluate the progress, and make periodic reports to the full worship committee. Another advantage of handling this work by subcommittee is that it will tend to attract more persons to the work by making someone other than the committee chairman responsible and it will create a long-term service project.

Fifth Action Meeting

See

Report and discuss any actions taken since the last meeting.

Can you recall the subject matter and petitions of any part of the Prayer of the Faithful that was read at last Sunday's Mass?

Who prepares the Prayer of the Faithful each week? Are commentators permitted to make changes and adaptations?

In your interviews and various discussions, has the Prayer of the Faithful been mentioned or discussed? Do you think people are aware of the Prayer of the Faithful?

Judge

What is your personal reaction to the Prayer of the Faithful as it is conducted in your worshipping community? Do you think it is an important part of the Mass? Discuss.

Do you think the Prayer of the Faithful is generally relevant to the needs and aspirations of yourself and your fellow parishioners? Is it usually very general in nature? Does it touch on racial reconciliation as it applies to your community?

Does this prayer give thanks for and celebrate the good things going on in your community? Does it deal with issues of peace, poverty, freedom, and other matters in terms of your community?

Do you think you and your fellow parishioners would talk to Christ personally about the same topics and in the same manner as that suggested by your Prayer of the Faithful? Why or why not?

WORSHIP

Act

Write below any suggested actions that developed from your discussion:

Do you see any need for changes in the way the Prayer of the Faithful is prepared and/or conducted? Why or why not?

If you see a need for change, what actions might be taken? If the Prayer of the Faithful is prepared by a diocesan office or by the pastor how can you make your viewpoints known most effectively? Write your suggestions here:

Is it possible for your committee to take responsibility for writing the Prayer of the Faithful? What would be the most effective way to handle such a project in order to make it representative of your worshipping community? Write your ideas here:

Helpful Questions: Is it possible that suggestions for the Prayer of the Faithful on Sunday be discussed at home Masses? Is it practical to allow a few minutes before Mass for parishioners to make known their needs and their blessings to be included in the Prayer of the Faithful? Is it possible to conduct the Prayer of the Faithful in such a way that parishioners might speak out during this period of the Mass to make known the blessings of God in their lives, their particular needs, and the needs of their relatives, friends, and neighbors? Do you have other ideas?

(Before you conclude this meeting: Set the topic, time, date, and place for your next meeting. Are there additional persons you should contact for membership in your committee at this time?)

6. Community Life

> He asked them, "How many loaves have you?" "Seven," they said.
> Then he instructed the crowd to sit down on the ground, and he took the seven loaves, and after giving thanks he broke them and handed them to his disciples to distribute; and they distributed them among the crowd. They had a few small fish as well, and over these he said a blessing and ordered them to be distributed also. They ate as much as they wanted, and they collected seven basketfuls of the scraps left over. Now there had been about four thousand people. He sent them away and immediately, getting into the boat with his disciples, went into the region of Dalmanutha.
>
> MARK 8:5-10

BECAUSE in today's pluralistic world there are an ever-increasing number of communities that affect the lives of each of us, the community life committee must be concerned with much more than the life of a single community. This parish council committee will help all the members of the worshipping community bring Christ to and make more human the multiplicity of communities in which they live, work, play, and have dealings with their fellow human beings. These communities will range from the parish and its immediate neighborhood to the city's central business district, from fraternal organizations to professional societies, from the local level to the national and international levels.

First Action Meeting

The purpose of these first two meetings is to build a general, factual picture of your parish. Because of the amount of research necessary, the meeting has been extended to two sessions. The first section deals only with the "see," or discovery, phase, while the second part of the meeting covers the judgment and action.

See

Do you have a map of the parish? Is it possible to obtain a large, wall-size parish map and a number of small copies of it?

What information does the latest census give for the neighborhoods within your parish boundaries?

What are the civic groups that meet within your parish boundaries?

Assign someone to draft a political map of your neighborhood. It should show the precincts, the ward, or other political boundaries that are within or encompass your parish. Accompanying this should be a list identifying every political office in the area and every official who lives within the parish boundaries or represents the people within the community, from the precinct captain to the U.S. senator.

Are there block groups or clubs of any kind within the parish boundaries? Indicate the locations of these groups on the map.

Where do people in your parish meet socially and informally? Only in and around the church? Are there parks, recreation areas, or shopping centers within your parish boundaries or nearby that are favored by the parishioners?

Where do the young people of the parish take their

dates? Where do they hang out? Are there coffee houses, pool halls, YMCA's, or other places in and nearby the parish? Do youth groups use the parish facilities?

Are there citizens' groups within the parish boundaries? A community organization? A PTA? A League of Women Voters? Are there civic and fraternal groups and business associations (Chamber of Commerce, Kiwanis, Knights of Columbus, etc.) that have halls and meetings in and nearby your parish?

Can you indicate on the map a general picture of the various traffic patterns within your parish? Is the church centrally located within the boundaries? How do the people get to church? Where do most of the people work, in terms of direction? How long is their commuting time?

What further questions can be asked now? What other information would committee members like to discover?

Hint: Much of the information asked for above is available in U.S. census reports and can be adapted to your particular boundaries or areas of concern by identifying the boundaries of the government "tracts." Also, there are in almost every city and town valuable resource persons (city hall officials, city planning officers, human relations experts, librarians, civic leaders, etc.) who can supply much of this information or refer you to previously prepared materials. Do not concern yourself with an in-depth, sciological study or the preparation of a detailed report. Your purpose is to get facts to see how much you know about your community and to get you acquainted with the character and issues of your community. In addition, you should become aware of the wealth of information that is usually available but not generally known by most members of the community.

In preparation for the next meeting: Does every member have a specific assignment? Do you know what you will be asked to report on?

Second Action Meeting

Each person should report on his research. His report should be prepared in writing, or a secretary should take down minutes of the reports as they are given.

Judge

What conclusions about your parish area can you draw from the research reported on?

Is the general pattern one of great confusion, with little interaction or chance for face-to-face contact among the parishioners? Or are there many opportunities for people to meet as neighbors and sharers of the same location and/or church?

Would you describe the neighborhoods in your parish as communities? Why or why not?

How would Christ judge a parish like this? What would he like about it? What would he dislike about it?

Act

Listed below are some *suggested* actions. Committee members themselves may now be prepared to suggest actions or may wish merely to list other possible actions or areas of action for later use.

Prepare the material you have gathered (with the parish map) in draft form to be duplicated and given to all the committee members and the council leadership.

Who else would be interested in your findings?

What further questions about your community might be asked now?

Should you assign a subcommittee to continue the job of researching facts about the parish and community, including histories and other references?

Would several other members like to interview community leaders, members of the real estate board, civic officials, and others to get their opinions on trends in the area and try to draw a picture of what your community might be like within five years?

Are committee members interested in talking with two other parishioners each, not members of the community life committee, about their findings? The conversation should be not only a report, but a request for additional information and their reactions to the study.

Write below other suggested actions and follow-up assignments:

Third Action Meeting

The community life committee may wish to meet for a buffet supper or covered-dish luncheon in preparation for this meeting. It should be held in a season of the year when people are moving about in their yards and in the streets. It should be held during daylight hours.

Following the meal, teams of two persons each are assigned to visit various areas within the parish boundaries. They are to talk with people they meet. They may wish to prepare a few sample questions to ask, but they should not run down a list of questions with the people they talk to, nor should they take notes while they are conducting what should be a casual interview.

The main purpose of their conversations should be to get acquainted with the persons they meet and find out whether they are happy. They will probably find it convenient to identify themselves as members of the parish council's community life committee who are trying to study the community. Most people are flattered to be asked their opinion and to discuss their own life in general terms of their length of time in the neighborhood, their work, and other facts.

The people you interview should be chosen at random. They need not be Catholic or members of your parish. All persons should be asked, however, whether they attend their church or synagogue regularly or irregularly. Does this affiliation or lack of it have any connection with their views of the neighborhood?

See

At least one hour and no more than two hours should be designated for the interviews. This will allow, with travel, time for one to three interviews.

If your community life committee has no more than twelve members, each team may report directly to the group. If your committee has more members, it would be better to break into two or more groups for the reporting sessions.

Teams should report their conversations as objectively as possible. A recording secretary should list the observations of each report. After all the teams have reported, a general discussion should be held.

Judge

What is your reaction to the various reports? Are people generally happy or unhappy with their neighborhoods? Why?

What issues or problems concern the people you talked with?

What kinds of responses would Christ make to the situations and people your interviews reveal?

Act

Do any of the interviews require a follow-up?

Should a summary of your reports be given to the pastor, the council leaders, and to other committees to aid them in their work?

Do any of the issues or concerns expressed in the interviews move you to discuss this program with other people not members of your committee?

Write below your suggested actions:

Fourth Action Meeting

See

Report and discuss the actions taken by members since your last meeting.

Who would you identify as the leaders of your community? Not only the political leaders, but the persons who head local organizations, and the persons to whom others turn for information and help?

How do things get done in your community? Who has the power? (Power might be described as money enough and people enough to get things done.)

Judge

How would you rate your community leadership? Is it good, bad, or indifferent in terms of the needs that you see for your community?

What do you see as the issues and the problems of your community? List them:

What do you think are the problems and issues that your community leaders see? List them:

Is there a lack of leadership in your community? Are there issues and problems not being tackled because there aren't enough leaders? What are the problems and issues that you have on the first list above that you did not include in the second list?

Act

Is there any action, or perhaps a number of actions, suggested by your discussion? If so, list them here:

Could each member of your committee interview one of the community leaders you have identified in your earlier discussions? Perhaps members could pair up and accompany each other on their interviews. During the interviews you might ask: "What do you see as the problems and issues of our community?" "Who do you think are the other leaders of this community?" "Is there a lack of leadership in the community?" "Do you think members of our parish are active enough in community affairs?" What other questions might you ask?

Could you assign persons to gather other information that will add to the data that you are collecting about your community? (It would be better to assign a number of people to parts of the tasks than to assign only one person.)

Are there persons you should invite to membership on the community life committee?

Fifth Action Meeting

See

If the interviews suggested in the previous meeting were conducted, have each member report on his interview. The report should be brief, factual, and informal, allowing other members to ask questions.

Were the interviews worthwhile? In what ways? Did they add to your knowledge about your community? Have the interviews changed your picture of your community? If so, in what ways? Were other leaders pointed out? Did you know them before? Did you recognize them as leaders before? What other problems and issues did the interviewees raise that you hadn't discussed before?

What other actions were taken by committee members? Ask them to report now. Discuss the reports.

Judge

Ask the secretary of your committee to read the minutes of your first meetings, especially the discussions concerning the judge sections. Do you detect any changes in your attitudes? If so, why? If you notice no changes, why do you suppose this is so?

Would Christ be pleased with a community like this? Why or why not? Answer both sections of the questions; list the good and bad views of your community:

Are there any changes in the list above from the answers you gave to a similar question in the second action meeting?

The next questions are personal. The members of your group should be well enough acquainted with each other at this time, however, to trust one another and treat each other with respect, understanding, and charity.

When did you move to this community? Can you recall why you selected this community? Are you as happy with, happier with, or less happy with your choice now? Why?

Would you consider yourself active or inactive in community affairs? Did you know personally any of the community leaders you discussed in these meetings before joining the community life committee? Were you aware of the problems and issues of your community before these meetings?

Act

Are you personally going to live in your community any differently as a result of these meetings? If so, describe the differences specifically.

How do you see the role of the community life committee in your parish and in your community? What should it be doing? Does our committee need more members to be effective? Does it need one or more subcommittees? What should they deal with?

How can the community life committee help your present community leaders do a more effective job?

If you feel there is a need for more leaders in your community, what can you do to help form leaders and involve other persons in the issues and problems of your community?

Can you help recruit members for community organizations and institutions? Can you cooperate with other groups to take a volunteer census and recruit persons needed for the community fund and health campaigns, for local hospitals, youth work, and the political parties? Can you cooperate with other groups to sponsor a community leadership course? (See Chapter 9 of *Parish Councils* for a program that might be adapted by your community.)

Plan your next meeting now. List below the actions agreed to in this meeting:

7. Education

"This, then, is what the parable means: the seed is the word of God. Those on the edge of the path are people who have heard it, and then the devil comes and carries away the word from their hearts in case they should believe and be saved. Those on the rock are people who, when they first hear it, welcome the word with joy. But these have no root; they believe for a while, and in time of trial they give up. As for the part that fell into the thorns, this is people who have heard, but as they go on their way they are choked by the worries and riches and pleasures of life and do not reach maturity. As for the part in the rich soil, this is people with a noble and generous heart who have heard the word and take it to themselves and yield a harvest through their perseverance."

LUKE 8:11-15

THE teaching function of the Church is one of the ministries of the bishop and of his representative, the local pastor; it is primarily with this function that the education committee of the parish council should involve itself. The education committee works not only with the parochial school board, the Home and School Association, and the CCD, but also with all those institutions which are seeking the truth and attempting to teach it. The committee's job is not to duplicate the efforts of other communities, but to open avenues of dialogue and cooperation between the worshipping community and all the varied educational communities around it.

First Action Meeting

Because of the extensive work needed to begin filling in a picture of the educational resources in your parish, this first meeting concentrates only on the observe or "see," while the judgment and action are contained in the second meeting. It would be helpful if a school board member (if you have a school board), the principal, and a parish priest would be present to help answer some of the questions which are probably not common knowledge in your worshipping community.

See

How many families are registered in your worshipping community? What is the total number of families living within the boundaries of your parish?

How many children attend the parochial school? What percentage is this amount of the number of children registered in your worshipping community? Where do those not in the parochial school attend school? What arrangements are made for religious instruction?

What about high school students? How many are there? Where do they attend school? What arrangements are made for their religious education?

How many children are there in each classroom of the parochial school? How does this compare with standards in the public school? Is there any method by which you can make a comparison or get facts on the quality of education in the parochial school? Has there been any recent self-study or evaluation?

Are there facilities and resources available for special education for children? What about physically handicapped children, the mentally retarded, and other exceptional children, including those with emotional problems and those with exceptional learning abilities?

Are Head Start and special tutoring programs offered at either the parochial or the public schools? How well attended and staffed are these projects? Are they sufficient for the needs of your community?

How much participation from the parents and the other members of the worshipping community is there in the policies of your parochial school? Are parents allowed to visit classrooms? Are there regular parent interviews? Is there a school board? Is there a Home and School Association?

Does the parish offer any type of regular educational programs for adults, including inquiry and information programs about the Catholic Church? Is there a program of study groups? Is there a library? Is there a "Coffee and Theology" or other lecture-discussion series?

Are you familiar with diocesan educational programs, including those that might be offered by the diocesan board of education, the liturgical commission, or adult education center? Are there diocesan family life programs, including Cana and the Christian Family Movement?

What other questions might be asked?

In preparation for the next meeting: It is not presumed that your committee will attempt a comprehensive educational directory, but your committee members should become aware of the resources, opportunities, and problems involved with all facets of education as it relates to your worshipping community and the persons in your parish area. Perhaps each member of your committee might conduct one, two, or three interviews before the next meeting, based on your discussion above. Discuss whom you might interview that would give you a fuller picture of educational needs and resources.

Second Action Meeting

See

Open the meeting with reports from each member. Have they obtained additional information on education in your parish? Who did they interview? What were the results? (The reports might be made in writing or the secretary might take minutes of each report.)

Judge

What is your general reaction to the reports? Discuss.

Were most of the people interviewed cooperative and interested? What do they feel are the good points and the problems involved in the educational programs available through your worshipping community?

Do you agree? What would you list as the positive points and what would you list as the problems involved with education in your parish?

Combine the lists of problems. Write them below:

How would you rate the problems in terms of priorities?

Are people of your area sufficiently aware of and making the fullest use of the educational programs? Why or why not?

EDUCATION

Act

Write below any action or actions that might have been suggested by your discussions:

Does your list above include school board members, Home-School officers, parents of children presently in the school, teachers, and persons with backgrounds in education who might not presently be involved with the parochial school or other parish educational projects?

Are there persons interviewed who indicated an interest in your committee and might be invited to become members? Are there other persons who might benefit from and add to the work of the committee if you invited them to join? Write below the names of the persons whom you will invite to the next meeting:

Would it help the work of your committee if a directory of your members and the various educational resource-people you have contacted be prepared and inexpensively reproduced for the use of committee members and other interested persons? Discuss what should be in the directory. Who will be responsible for preparing and distributing the directory?

In preparation for the next meeting: Look at the "See" questions in the Third Action Meeting. How many can you answer now? Would it be possible to assign members to get answers to certain questions?

Third Action Meeting

See

Report and discuss actions taken since the last meeting.

What public school district is your parish in? What are the schools and locations to which members of your community go?

Who are the principals and school officials? Are there active PTA's in these schools? Who are the leaders in these institutions?

Are there specialized educational institutions (e.g., Montessori schools, nursery schools, etc.) in your community?

Are there universities, colleges, and junior colleges, both public and private, in your community?

Judge

Are the schools adequate for your community needs? How would you rate each school?

Are the classes overcrowded? Is the curriculum geared to the needs of today's students and the special needs of the community?

Are minority members represented among the pupils and the faculty?

Are community members able to make their voices heard in the policy decisions of the board of education and the individual schools? How?

What would you say are the chief issues and problems in your public schools?

Why should parish members, including parents who have their children in parochial schools, be interested in the public school system?

EDUCATION

Act

Write below any actions that might have been suggested by your discussion:

Are any of your committee members active in the public school system—on the board of education, on the faculty, or with the Parent-Teacher Association? Should they be active? If you do not have active representation from the public school system, is it possible that some of your members may wish to run for board of education offices or become active in the PTA? Can you have a representative of the education committee attend and report on each meeting of the board of education? Can you enlist membership on your education committee from persons who are presently active within the public school system? Write any actions agreed upon here:

Can members of the education committee interview various representatives of the public school system to learn more about it? The interviewees might be board of education members, principals, faculty members, PTA leaders, and a number of parents of public school children. What issues and problems do the interviewees see with your school-district education? Write below your assignments for interviews:

Fourth Action Meeting

See

Each member should report on any action or actions taken since the last meeting.

If interviews were made, brief reports should be given by each member. Discuss them fully.

Judge

Reviewing your first three meetings, how would you define the purpose of your education committee? Is it developing the way you would like to see it go? Are you dealing with issues and problems and getting in contact with other persons not members of your committee?

What has your committee accomplished to date? Are your members taking the actions agreed to and the interviews?

What about the makeup of your committee? Are you representative of your worshipping community? Do you have enough members to take the actions and do the interviews that you feel are necessary? Are the members still enthusiastic? Why or why not?

Act

Write below the action or actions that might have been suggested from your discussion:

EDUCATION

Are there services in terms of education that the committee might take on or encourage other parish and community groups to sponsor or co-sponsor? These might include an educational directory, a tutoring program, the organizing of a Montessori school, etc. What other services are needed in your community? List them:

Can the education committee put on a program to inform the entire community of the issues and problems in your public school district and in the parochial school? Perhaps the purpose of the meeting might be to encourage active participation from the parishioners by actively recruiting membership on the education committee, on the parochial school board, in the Home and School Association, in the local Parent-Teacher Associations, and in other such groups. Write below your suggestions for such a program:

Might some of these groups be willing to co-sponsor or cooperate in putting on an educational fair, in which booths are manned to give information on specific programs, to sign up registrants for various adult and specialized education courses, and solicit membership in the Home and School Association, PTA, and other groups?

Fifth Action Meeting

See

Ask for reports of actions taken since the last meeting. Discuss.

Judge

For the last few meetings you have been dealing with institutions and more formal means of learning. What other ways of learning are there? List some other ways that man learns in today's world, including television, newspapers, and magazines:

Should a Christian group, such as your education committee, be concerned not only about religious education, but every increase in man's knowledge? Discuss.

A function of education is to develop man's critical ability. There are informal programs, such as discussion groups, the Great Books and Junior Great Books programs, that can help to develop this critical faculty. Is there anything that the education committee might do to promote this type of education?

Act

Write below any suggested action or actions growing from your reports and discussion:

EDUCATION

It is difficult for man to exercise his critical ability under a constant barrage of electronic media, especially if he does not understand the new media. Is it possible that a discussion or a series of discussions might be held on the effects of mass media? Could speakers be contacted who might be willing to lead discussions on such topics as "How To Read A Newspaper"? The public service departments of your newspapers, radio stations, and television outlets may have resources for you. The journalism and communications departments of local colleges would be helpful, too. If you have a diocesan bureau of information, contact the staff for help and ideas. Write your plan of action below, if this action is agreed to by the group:

An unusual educational offering of guided tours might be offered in cooperation with the community life, social committee, and other groups in the parish and community. Many people who never make use of art institutes and museums can be introduced to these wonderful cultural and educational facilities through guided tours. In the same way, an experienced community leader might conduct a bus tour of your area and be able to awaken in you a new awareness of the persons, opportunities, and issues around you. Would these or similar ideas be practical projects for your education committee? Write your plans or other ideas below:

Plan your next meeting now. What will be the topic of discussion? Where and when will the meeting be held? Be sure to ask for reports of actions.

8. Apostolate

> He called the Twelve together and gave them power and authority over all devils and to cure diseases, and he sent them out to proclaim the kingdom of God and to heal.
>
> He said to them, "Take nothing for the journey, neither staff, nor haversack, nor bread, nor money; and let none of you take a spare tunic. Whatever house you enter, stay there; and when you leave, let it be from there. As for those who do not welcome you, when you leave their town shake the dust from your feet as a sign to them."
>
> So they set out and went from village to village proclaiming the Good News and healing everywhere.
>
> LUKE 9:1-6

CHRIST sent his disciples to tell of the coming of the kingdom of God. The modern Christian community continues his work by sending disciples to tell of the Good News. Promoting and encouraging participation by members of the worshipping community in the apostolic work of the Church, the apostolic committee opens up the parochial boundaries of the parish to the neighborhood, the city, the country, and the world, and the universe.

The concerns of this committee are as broad of those of the Church itself and can find expression through work with the many existing organizations of specialized and general Catholic Action, as well as through new initiatives that will meet the special needs and unique conditions facing the Church in a secularized, pluralistic world.

First Action Meeting

See

What does it mean to be apostolic?

Can you give examples of persons who have an apostolic zeal?

List the apostolic activities in your parish.

Judge

Have you personally ever invited someone to join the Catholic Church? Have you ever talked with someone about Christ? Discuss.

Is a program of "making converts" outmoded in this era of ecumenical good will? Why or why not?

What apostolic activities are you now engaged in or have you been active in recently?

How do you think Christ, as one who sent his apostles to spread his message about the coming of the kingdom of God, would judge your parish?

What is this kingdom of God that Christ talked about? Where is it? When is it coming? Do we have to do anything about it?

APOSTOLATE

Act

Write below the action or actions suggested by your discussion:

Would your group find it helpful to schedule another meeting, before going on, to discuss Chapter Two of this book, "Christian Formation"? Discussion questions are provided as a guide at the end of the chapter along with suggested additional reading. Or, perhaps you might take one of the books mentioned in the resources section following Chapter Two as your discussion material. Write the date, time, place, and the agreed topic if you decide to follow through on this suggested action:

Would you find it profitable to schedule an Afternoon of Recollection? Perhaps one of the priests of the parish, or another priest recommended by one of your committee members, might lead conferences on "The Mission of Christ," "The Kingdom of God," or "You Are An Apostle." Could a general invitation be extended to the parish to participate? Who might you personally invite? If you decide to schedule this Afternoon of Recollection, list below the date, time, and place; the chairman and subcommittee responsible for arrangements; and the persons that you personally will invite:

Second Action Meeting

See

Report on any actions accomplished since the last meeting.

If one or both of the meetings suggested in the first action meeting were agreed to, what progress has been made in arrangements?

What opportunities do your relatives, neighbors, and friends have to learn of Christ? List the ways and means that are available to them.

Judge

Would you say that most of the people who live in your community have an adequate opportunity to learn of Christ and his message? Why or why not?

What other ways and means that you know of are not available in your parish?

Act

List below the action or actions suggested by your discussion:

APOSTOLATE

Is it possible for each member of the apostolic committee to interview a person in your community who is not affiliated with any church or synagogue? The interview should be brief. Be sure to pledge to keep the person's identity unknown. Ask the person if he can recall when he first heard about Christ. Was he ever affiliated with any church? If so, why did he leave? What type of church, if any, would he now affiliate with, given the opportunity? Has he been invited to join a church since he moved to this community? What other questions might be asked? Would it be helpful if a brief questionnaire were prepared? Should interviewers carry a letter of introduction from the apostolic committee? Might other parishioners be asked to take part in this survey? Write your plan of action below:

Helpful hints and questions: Would another brief meeting prior to the survey help? In this way, instructions might be given in the use of the survey form. Would role-playing help those persons who feel ill at ease about such interviews? What about sending the interviewers out two-by-two? Do any interviewers need help to find persons not presently active with a church? "Cold calls" might be made, in which the interviewer introduces himself and directly asks the person who answers the door whether he is presently active in a church. If he is active, ask him to recommend a neighbor who is not.

Third Action Meeting

See

Report on all actions taken since the last meeting. Discuss.

Report and discuss the interviews with persons not affiliated with any church.

Judge

What did you learn from the interviews? Are there more or are there fewer people than you had imagined who have not heard about Christ or who have heard very little about him? Are there fewer or more people than you had imagined who are not now affiliated with a church?

Had most of the people been contacted by one or more people to join a church since they had moved into the community?

Were most of the people you interviewed aware of your parish? Had they ever been contacted by a priest or a member of your parish? Did they recall the visit? Was their impression favorable? Had there been any follow-up? Discuss in detail.

Act

Write below any action or actions that might be suggested by your discussions:

Can you make your information available in a report to the priests of the parish and the council? Would members of the local ministerial association or Church federation benefit from a copy of your report?

Has the ministerial association or your parish a welcoming committee for new residents, so that they might be referred to the church of their choice? How does such a program work? Is there adequate follow-up and is it done in a personal way? If there is not such a program, can the apostolic committee promote it? Can it be done in cooperation with the community life committee, other community groups, and the local ministerial association? If you wish to pursue this idea, write your plan of action below:

Has a complete census of your area been done in cooperation with your parish and the local ministerial association? In the light of your interviews is a program needed? Does your experience in the interviews suggest ways to make the census effective? Perhaps the leadership for the apostolic committee could meet with the parish priests, the community life committee, and the ministerial association officers to discuss the possibility of a full community survey. If this is practical, write your plan of action below:

Look at the "See" questions for the next meeting. Can interviews be assigned so that these questions are answered? It would be well to talk with the pastor and other persons active with the inquiry classes.

Fourth Action Meeting

See

Report and discuss all actions taken since the last meeting.
How often are inquiry classes conducted in your parish?
How are they conducted? What materials (e.g., textbooks, audio-visual materials, etc.) are used for the course?
How many persons generally attend an inquiry class? What percentage are later baptized and/or received into the Church?

Judge

If you were not a member of the parish would you have been attracted to the Church through an invitation to your parish's inquiry class? Why or why not?
Have you ever invited someone to the inquiry class? What were the results? Have you been active in the conduct of the class? Have you ever visited the inquiry class?
Are people greeted warmly in the inquiry class? Do persons attending the inquiry classes have plenty of opportunities to talk personally with the priests and people of the parish? Are they given the feeling that they are joining a Christian community? Are they introduced to the community or given a chance to participate in the community before they complete the classes?
What type of follow-up program is conducted? Is there follow-up with both those who are received into the Church and with those who elect not to join? Discuss.

APOSTOLATE

Act

Write below the action or actions that might be suggested by your discussion:

Is there anything that the apostolic committee might do to improve the inquiry classes? Would it be possible for the apostolic committee to work with the priests and the council leadership to take responsibility for the conduct of the inquiry classes, including recruiting, hosting, teaching, and follow-up? Write your plan of action here:

Would inquiry or information classes held at the same time as other programs in the other Christian churches of the community solicit more support? Can such a joint program be worked out, with a community-wide recruiting program, but with each church conducting their own inquiry classes and follow-up? What do you see as the advantages and disadvantages of this type of program? Discuss.

Can you get names and addresses of previous participants in your parish inquiry program, interview them, and get suggestions for improvement in the classes and follow-up for the inquiry program?

When are convert baptisms held? Would it help to have public baptisms at one of the Sunday masses, and especially during the Easter Season? Discuss.

Fifth Action Meeting

See

What groups in the parish are presently offering Christian formation? List them, and then discuss how they give apostolic formation:

What other groups *not* now in the parish are available to give Christian formation? List them:

Have you included, in either list above, the Young Christian Students (grade school, high school, college divisions), Christian Family Movement, Cursillo, Legion of Mary, various Third Orders, Young Christian Movement? What do you know about these groups?

Judge

Why is it important that persons belong to small groups to receive Christian formation? Isn't it enough that they attend regular parish worship services and functions? Discuss.

APOSTOLATE

Act

List below the action or actions that might have been suggested by your discussions:

Are there representatives on your apostolic committee from each of the groups in your parish who are engaged in Christian formation? Would it be valuable to have such representation? Can you discuss and recruit such membership? List your assignments below:

Are you familiar with all the various groups engaged in Christian formation that were listed in your discussion? How might you learn more about them? One possibility for such an action might be for each member of the apostolic committee to interview one leader from each of the various groups and report back at a future meeting. Where the group is not represented in the parish, perhaps an interview might be held with a person who is active with the group in another parish or who is concerned with the diocesan office of the group. *The National Catholic Almanac* will give national offices for most of the groups.

Prepare now for the next meeting. When, where, and at what time will it be held? What will be the topic of discussion? Be sure to open with reports of actions. Who else should be invited to the meeting? List these details here:

If you do not have a topic for your next meeting, you might consider an evaluation of your progress to date. Discuss the enthusiasm of your group, the accomplishments, and the failures. Is your committee growing? Are members completing the actions they agree to do? Are friendships being formed? Have you undertaken service projects?

9. Family Life

> His mother and brothers now arrived and, standing outside, sent in a message asking for him. A crowd was sitting round him at the time the message was passed to him, "Your mother and brothers and sisters are outside asking for you."
>
> He replied, "Who are my mother and my brothers?" And looking round at those sitting in a circle about him, he said, "Here are my mother and my brothers. Anyone who does the will of God, that person is my brother and sister and mother."
>
> MARK 3:31-35

RECOGNIZING the many conditions in today's world that adversely affect family life, and concerned about the good of all the persons among whom they live, whether these persons are members of the worshipping community or not, the members of the family life committee work to make the conditions of family life more human and to strengthen that life in Christ. Issues in society that affect the family; relationships between husband and wife and between parents and children; opportunities for family action in apostolic and social affairs: these and many other items can find a place on the agenda of this committee.

Cooperating with other parish council committee, diocesan programs, and with secular agencies, the family life committee can work not only for happier families, but for expansive families whose doors are open to receive everyone in the name of Christ.

First Action Meeting

See

How many families do you know in the parish? How many additional families do you know in the community area?

Would you say that most, many, or few of these families have a good life together? Are they able to meet their problems? Would you say that they have great love and concern for each other, or do they appear merely to be a collection of persons who happen to sleep under the same roof?

Judge

What is your definition of a good family life? Discuss.

Would you say that your parish is a family-centered one? Why or why not?

Is your community a good one in which to raise a family? List the things in your community that are positive supports for family life:

List the things in your community that hinder or prevent full family life:

FAMILY LIFE

Act

Write here any suggestions for action growing from your discussion:

Before the next meeting could you discuss the above questions with a number of other couples? This might be done informally, or you might host a brief discussion at your home. The aim of the conversation might be to define a good family life, not in an academic way, but by what it means personally to those with whom you talk.

Is your family life committee large enough to be effective? Who else might be invited to membership? Perhaps a number of persons that you interview, if you elect to do the above action, will show an interest in the family life committee.

Has the discussion above intrigued you enough to find out more about family life programs that might be offered in your parish, in your community, in your diocese, and in the metropolitan area? Who might you talk with or where could you go to get more information?

Would it be well to talk with social workers, parish priests, ministers, and family counselors to get ideas about the quality of family life in your community? Write your further ideas and your assignment here.

Second Action Meeting

See

Where do families "in trouble" go for help in your parish and your community? If a husband or wife had a drinking problem and talked with you, what would you recommend? Discuss. Are there families in your community that need financial help? Have you ever noticed senior citizens buying cat and dog food when they don't have a pet? Have you ever noticed children who do not have adequate clothes or lunch money? How can you be aware of signs of poverty and financial difficulty around you and who, if anyone, helps these people now?

What does a mother with small children do who is divorced or whose husband has left her? How does she support the children? Does she have a job skill? How are the children being cared for while she is working? Is there any other way to solve the problem? What funds might be available to her? What agencies can you refer her to, and how much of the problem can they help her with?

What about families that are together, but fight constantly and probably need professional counseling? Are there such services available? Where? How can they learn about these services? What role can you play?

Is there any help for a couple who are struggling to raise a number of small children and who fear another pregnancy?

Judge

What would Christ want us to do about these problems?

FAMILY LIFE

Do we always have the competence to deal with the problems we see? What then is our responsibility? Discuss specific examples.

Can we assume that there are enough agencies to offer help and that all families are capable of meeting problems or eventually finding aid?

Act

What action or actions might be suggested by your discussion? Write them below:

List below all the persons, institutions, and agencies that might be available in your community to help families in trouble:

Is there an agency directory available? If not, can one be drawn up? Can members of your committee interview persons from the agencies to find out the type of family problems in your community and what help is available? Write your assignments below:

Third Action Meeting

See

Report on any actions taken since the last meeting. Discuss them fully.

Judge

What would you say are the principal problems that families experience in your area? Are there adequate resources to meet them? What other resources are needed?

Doesn't every family have problems? List some of the typical problems that families have. Be specific. What are some of the problems you have experienced in your family life? Would other families profit from the retelling of such experiences?

Do you think young people are given adequate preparation for marriage? Are there programs in the parish, the high school, or in college that can help them? Detail the programs and discuss their value.

Are pre-Cana programs offered in your parish and diocese? Are they well attended? Are they helpful? Are non-Catholics invited?

Act

Write below any suggested action or proposed service that your committee might do in the area of family life:

Might the family life committee sponsor pre-Cana or other marriage preparation courses for engaged couples from your community? If you agree, write your action plan below:

If non-Catholic couples are invited, how should the course content be arranged? Couldn't questions of Catholic marriage discipline be confined to one session, with the sacramental view of marriage being presented throughout all the sessions? What other details might have to be arranged?

Can your committee sponsor a Cana program or a family-centered Day of Recollection followed with a social or buffet supper? If you agree, write your action plan here:

Are there services that you have discovered the need for that might be further explored and then acted upon?

Is there a need for a credit union in the parish to help families with their budgeting and to save wasted dollars in interest on car purchases and in revolving credit accounts?

Is it possible to create an exchange program for baby items that are outgrown before they wear out? The parish bulletin might be used to list baby carriages, clothing, and other items that are serviceable and that could be purchased at a nominal price, loaned, or "rented out."

Could a baby-sitting service be established?

Fourth Action Meeting

See

Report on any interviews and actions taken since the last meeting. Discuss them fully.

Does your parish have a children's Mass?

Are parents permitted to receive Communion with their children when they make their First Communion? Is the family involved in the preparation of their children for First Communion?

Is there an active Christian Family Movement in the parish? Is there a parents' club? Are there separate men's and women's clubs in the parish?

Are men as well as women active in the Home and School Association or other group related to the parochial school?

Judge

How would you answer the questions raised in the judge section in the first meeting of this chapter? Review the questions and discuss them now. Do you notice any changes in your own or the group's attitudes?

Is it good that a parish be family-centered? Do you think your parish should be less or more family-centered than it is now? Why?

Act

Write below any actions that would be suggested by your discussion:

FAMILY LIFE

Are you familiar with the ecumenical program of the Christian Family Movement? Is there a CFM group in your parish? If so, do you have CFM couples as members of your family life committee? If you do not have a CFM group in your parish, would you be interested in learning more about its program? If so, who will be responsible for asking for information on CFM, contacting a nearby group, or inviting CFM representation on your committee?

What type of family programs do the churches and synagogues in your area offer? Is it possible that you might have a meeting with such groups similar to yours to discuss family life in the community? Write your plan of action here:

Do you have persons not members of your worshipping community as members of your family life committee? Should you have? What are the advantages and disadvantages? Discuss. If you agree to pursue this possible action, what next steps need to be taken?

Read over the questions and comments now for the next meeting. Is there anything you should do in preparation for the meeting? If so, write it below, along with the date, time, and place of the meeting:

Fifth Action Meeting

See

Report any actions taken since the last meeting. Discuss them fully.

Has your committee begun any regular service program to families of the parish and the community? What is it? What remains to be done? Discuss.

Judge

Why should the family life committee be engaged in a service project or program to the families and the community? Discuss.

How would you define the family life committee? Is it a necessary committee in your parish council?

Act

Note below any action or actions that have been agreed to as a result of the discussion above:

How is your family life committee represented on the parish council board? Do you work with other committees and parish groups? Discuss this cooperation. Might you help the education committee with home-and-school lecture-discussions on such topics as sex education, drugs, and family communication? Where else might you help?

Have you been able to make your views on family life in your community heard by the various agencies and leaders of your community? What would you say is your most important action or contribution to family life in your community to date? Why? What other needs are there? What else might you do? Write your suggestions below:

Might other persons be invited to join your committee? Who?

Are you still working with your directory of family-related agencies? Have you made additions to it lately? Could copies be reproduced and distributed to families in the parish and in the community?

Is there a need in your community for more trained and professional family counselors? Where is such training available? Can you help recruit likely prospects for such training? Are any members of your committee interested in pursuing such work? List any possible actions in this area below:

What time, day, and place will you meet next? After you report your actions, what topic or topics will you discuss?

10. Social

> He then told the guests a parable, because he had noticed how they picked the places of honor. He said this, "When someone invites you to a wedding feast, do not take your seat in the place of honor. A more distinguished person than you might have been invited, and the person who invited you both may come and say, 'Give up your place to this man.' And then, to your embarrassment, you would have to go and take the lowest place. No; when you are a guest, make your way to the lowest place and sit there, so that, when your host comes, he may say, 'My friend, move up higher.' In that way, everyone with you at the table will see you honored. For everyone who exalts himself will be humbled, and the man who humbles himself will be exalted."
>
> LUKE 14:7-11

THE organizer and arranger of social events for members of the worshipping community, the social life committee tries to promote friendships among the various members and to encourage their active participation in the social and cultural life of the varied communities around them. It can promote that community feeling that is so necessary to effective corporate worship, expand the visions of individuals and families in their use of leisure time, and, generally, promote that social intercourse from which the family of Christ might be formed.

First Action Meeting

See

Would you describe your parish as warm and friendly? Why or why not?

Relate your own experiences on moving into your present home. Did anyone welcome you? Did you register in the parish? If so, how was the registration conducted? Was there any follow-up? Were you given adequate information about the worshipping community and items of interest in the community?

Does your parish have a program to greet newcomers and to help them get acquainted in the parish and the community?

What opportunities do people have to get to know other persons in the parish and community? Is there an active recruiting program by the parish council committees and other parish groups? How does a person learn about other community groups and events? List some of the ways:

Judge

Is it necessary that a parish develop a feeling of fellowship? Isn't it just as well that Masses begin on time and that people are able to move quickly in and out of the church and the parking lot and back to their own affairs? Is this what they want? Discuss.

Pretend that Christ visited your parish unannounced. Discuss what would happen. (Let yourself go! A humorous approach will probably work better than a serious one.)

Is the above suggestion really so strange? Why or why not?

SOCIAL

Act

Write below any action or actions suggested by your discussion:

Could each committee member interview two persons from the parish? Discuss with them the questions in the "See" section above. Report on the conversations at the next meeting. Do you know two recent arrivals in the parish?

Look at a map of your parish. Does your parish have areas that are at odds with each other or that do not communicate with each other? For example, some parishes in communities divided by railroad tracks, expressways, or other barriers often find it difficult to express a sense of unity among parishioners. If this is true in your case what can be done about it?

Would people in your parish welcome the chance to meet more often and informally? Would a regular Sunday program of coffee, juice, and rolls served in the church hall or other convenient location provide an opportunity for people to meet, get to know each other, and thus develop more concern for each other? Could the social committee take on this or a similar project as a regular service? Discuss. Write your plan of action:

Second Action Meeting

See

Report on any actions and interviews taken since the last meeting. Discuss them in full.
What issues and problems did the persons you talk with reveal? Are they something that the social committee should act upon? Should some of them be referred to other persons, other parish council committees, or other community groups?
List below all the parish council committees and parish organizations. After each one, list a contact person and phone number, and a brief description of what the committee or group does or is concerned about:

Judge

Is your list complete? What groups do you need more information on? Who else might you check with to see that your list is comprehensive?
Is this information generally known in the parish?

SOCIAL

Act

Write below the action or actions suggested by your discussion:

Does the social committee have representation from other parish organizations? Are there other organizations that might be represented through a member or two serving on the social committee? Write your plan of action below:

Are there committees and organizations which are not represented in your parish which serve a need for persons of your worshipping community?

Would it be possible for members of the social committee to call on newly registered members of the parish? Should a chairman and a subcommittee be assigned to this project as a continuing service? Discuss the purposes of such a service and how it might work. Write your plan of action below:

Third Action Meeting

See

How would you describe your community? Is it warm and friendly? Why or why not?

Is it open to all persons regardless of race, color, and creed? Are various ages, educational backgrounds, and income groups represented?

Does everyone have a chance to voice their opinion in the community, through council meetings, board of education meetings, etc.? Is there a community organization?

Are there many active and varied organizations in your community? What types of activities are offered? What types of needs are met through such free associations? Are they open to all in the community?

Judge

Do people buy a home like a car, or do they really care about the setting of their family life and look for a friendly, responsive community? Discuss.

List below all of the community groups in which you and members of your committee are presently active (including the community organization, block club, Great Books, Kiwanis, Chamber of Commerce, community orchestra, etc.):

SOCIAL

Are people of all types, including young people with long hair, accepted and treated with respect in your community? Discuss.

Would Christ be accepted in your community? Remember, he's Jewish. Would he be accepted if he were bearded and dressed as most pictures paint him? Would he be accepted if he were clean-shaven and in a business suit?

Act

Write below the action or actions suggested by your discussion:

Are the community groups that members of your committee belong to fairly representative of the groups available in your community? What other groups are there that you have heard about?

Could members of the social committee find and talk with members of other groups not mentioned and report on them in the next meeting? The community life committee members, the local community newspaper, and other known community leaders would be able to help you get acquainted with persons from other groups in the community. Write your assignment here:

Fourth Action Meeting

See

Report any actions taken and new information on parish and community groups gained since the last meeting. Discuss.

Judge

Has your image of the parish changed in any way since your first meeting with the social committee? Has your image of the community changed in any way? Describe and discuss.

Do you think other people of the parish and of the community are aware of the various persons, groups, and resources that you have now discovered in your area? Would it be good for them to become familiar with these? Discuss.

Discuss how the work of your committee can make life more human and more Christ-like for the other members of the worshipping community and the other persons of your area.

Act

Write below the suggested action or actions growing from your discussions:

SOCIAL

Is it possible that the information you have gathered about parish and community groups might be broadcast more widely? Can you discuss it with members of the council board and other committees, such as community life, that might have similar concerns? Write your assignment below:

Can a directory be made from your list of parish and community groups and events, to be distributed yearly and to be given to new members of your worshipping community? Could the directory serve an even wider audience through cooperation with other parish council committees and other community groups? Could it be given to all newcomers to the area? Which groups should you work with to produce the directory and get it distributed? Write your plan of action below:

Have you thought about surveying the various cultural and recreational facilities of your community? Wouldn't it be useful to have these included in a directory? Could members survey such opportunities before the next meeting? The survey might include the parks, swimming pools, movie houses, community theater, etc. Write your assignment here:

Fifth Action Meeting

See

Report any actions taken since the last meeting. Discuss.

Judge

Have the secretary read the minutes from your previous meetings. Each member might comment on his reaction and his evaluation of the social committee and its progress to date.

Has your social committee grown in membership and enthusiasm since the first meeting? Discuss. Be specific.

Is your social committee representative of your worshipping community and your area? Discuss how it is representative. List ways it could be more representative:

Have you taken on a service project for the parish and the community? If so, evaluate its progress.

Have the members of the social committee developed friendships and concerns among themselves? Have you developed friendships and concerns with other persons that you have met in the parish and the community through your various actions and interviews?

How do you think Christ would evaluate your committee's work?

SOCIAL

Act

Write below the action or actions suggested by your discussion:

Could the social committee hold a newcomers' party every month or every three months, depending upon the need? Might this be co-sponsored with other committees (e.g., community life, family life) and other groups? A brief program might be designed to introduce new families and persons to the worshipping community and to the various activities and opportunities available through the parish council committees and organizations and the community resources. Write your plan of action:

Are persons of your community fully aware and taking advantage of the various programs offered by your worshipping community, other churches, the park districts, etc.? What can you do to help these programs? Write suggestions here:

Are there worthwhile programs that might be offered if various leaders, community groups, and institutions were aware of the needs that you have discovered? Are park district hours convenient? Would selected movies and discussions attract a sufficient number of people to pay a local movie theater to schedule them? Would lecture-discussions on issues of our day be a worthwhile project for the local library or several community groups to co-sponsor? Would a special program on leisure opportunities spark some creative approaches and cause new lines of communication and cooperation to be opened in your community? Is there an historic event or special community event that might be commemorated with a day of festivities and thus help to give expression to community fellowship? Might these ideas be pursued at your next meeting? Plan now for your next meeting. Write below the topic, time, date, and place:

11. Finance and Administration

> Last came forward the man who had the one talent. "Sir," said he, "I had heard you were a hard man, reaping where you have not sown and gathering where you have not scattered; so I was afraid, and I went off and hid your talent in the ground. Here it is; it was yours, you have it back." But his master answered him, "You wicked and lazy servant! So you knew that I reap where I have not sown and gather where I have not scattered? Well, then, you should have deposited my money with the bankers, and on my return I would have recovered my capital with interest. So now, take the talent from him and give it to the man who had the five talents. For to everyone who has will be given more, and he will have more than enough; but from the man who has not, even what he has will be taken away."
>
> MATTHEW 25:23–29

OCCUPIED with the financing, properties, and administration of the parish, the finance and administration committee arranges for the Christ-like and most efficient use of the money and physical properties of the worshipping community. Through its works, which often demand special competence in law, accounting, and administration, this committee can free priests for more pastoral work and emphasize anew the importance of persons over stones in the building up of the Church.

First Action Meeting

See

What has been the history of finances and administration in your parish? Has it always been the sole concern of the pastor? Discuss.

Does your parish have any trustees? Who are they? Are they members of your committee?

Does your parish issue an annual financial report?

How is parish property held? How are finances handled? Does your diocese have strong central arrangements for the handling of funds, insurance, and purchases? How much choice is exercised by your pastor?

Do you know how other parish councils handle matters of finance and administration? Are you familiar with such arrangements in Protestant Churches? How does it agree with or differ from the manner in which finances and administration are handled in the Catholic Church?

Judge

Do you believe there is a need for a change in the present finance and administration of your parish? Why or why not?

Are these changes necessary to implement and to give fuller expression to community concepts? Discuss.

Act

What action or actions are suggested by your discussion? Write the specifics below:

FINANCE AND ADMINISTRATION

Is it possible to get a complete financial accounting and a list of all properties in the parish? Who will undertake the assignment?

Is your finance and administration committee adequately staffed? Do you have enough members as you see the scope of your work now? Are your members representative of the parish? Do you have a number of members who have professional competence (e.g., lawyers, public accountants) in some of the areas you will be dealing with? Write your plan of action here:

Can members of your committee visit other parish councils and other churches to talk with leaders and see how they handle finance and administration concerns? Write your assignments below:

Second Action Meeting

See

Report all actions and interviews since the last meeting. Discuss.

Do you have a complete financial picture of the parish? How do the finances and properties of your worshipping community relate to the finances and administration of your first pastor, the bishop? What information is available from your diocesan offices?

Do you have case histories, samples of annual reports, and interviews with other parish councils and churches?

(Pass what samples you have among the members. Ask them to evaluate the materials. Are they attractive? Are they understandable? What techniques were used in reporting? Do any of the reports tie in the financial and administrative affairs of the church with community concepts, the mission of the Church, etc.?)

Judge

Is an annual report for the parish necessary? Why or why not?

If you have an annual report, should it be concerned only with finances and administration?

What are the advantages of presenting a complete and full annual report to the entire worshipping community? List them:

What are the disadvantages of presenting such a report? List them:

FINANCE AND ADMINISTRATION

Act

Write below the suggested action or actions growing from your discussion:

If you elect to prepare an annual report, should it be presented both in writing and also orally at the annual meeting of the assembly of the parish council or at another time when the full parish is gathered?

What else might be included in the annual report, along with the financial statement and other matters of administration? Have you discussed this with parish council board members and with other committee leaders?

Can members of the finance and administration committee interview heads of corporations, public relations consultants, community organization executive directors, and others to get further samples of annual reports and tips on their preparation and use? Write your assignments here:

How else might the annual report be used? Have you considered using it as an information booklet to be given to newly registered members of your worshipping community? Might copies be presented to other community leaders, so that civic officials, business leaders, other church ministers and leaders, and various other opinion leaders will understand the purpose and work of your worshipping community?

Third Action Meeting

See

Report on all interviews and actions taken since the last meeting. Discuss.

If additional samples of annual reports have been obtained since the last meeting, pass them among the members, and discuss.

Do you have a budget for the coming fiscal year? How is the budget for your worshipping community drawn up? Are council board members and individual committee members consulted? Are open hearings held on the proposed budget?

Is the accounting for such a budget in line with the accounting for the annual report? Is it understandable? Is responsibility for specific budget items, including income and expenses, clearly pinpointed?

Judge

Does your budget indicate that your worshipping community is meeting its obligations in a Christian way? Are provisions for an adequate family income made for all lay personnel? Are priests and religious compensated justly?

Is hiring done on an equal opportunity basis?

Are provisions made in the budget for health and accident insurance and retirement programs for both religious and lay persons?

Are teachers and other parish workers members of unions? Are they prevented from joining?

Would Christ be happy with the way that your worshipping community expresses its purpose, fulfills its obligations, and contributes to the Church and the world, as shown by your annual report and budget?

FINANCE AND ADMINISTRATION

Act

Write below the suggested action or actions from your discussion:

Would it be more efficient to have a subcommittee work out a budget in cooperation with the pastor, the council officers, and committee leaders and report back to the full committee? If so, list the chairman and subcommittee members here:

Do you have enough members to carry out your responsibilities? Is your membership representative of your worshipping community? Are all of the members of your worshipping community aware of your work and progress?

Preview the next meeting. If your annual report does not contain a list of all the parish properties and facilities, can several members be assigned that task in preparation for the next meeting? Write the date, time, and place of the next meeting, with your assignment:

Fourth Action Meeting

See

Report on all actions and interviews since the last meeting. Discuss, including further follow-through and assignments if needed.

List below the number of hours that each of your parish facilities is actually used out of the 168 hours in each week:

Church proper:
Church hall:
Rectory meeting room(s):
Parish hall:
School hall:
Other:

Judge

Are your parish facilities adequately and efficiently used? How does their use compare with the use of other buildings of other churches and parishes? How efficient is their use compared with commercial and public buildings?

Are your church facilities adequate to meet the needs of your worshipping community? Are parish groups prevented from using meeting space in the parish because the facilities are not adequate? Are community groups not able to use parish facilities because of the lack of space and a crowded schedule?

What is the parish policy on the use of its facilities? How does one go about securing the use of the parish hall? Must the pastor's permission be secured in each case? Are fees charged? Is the policy just and flexible enough for the needs of groups of the worshipping com-

FINANCE AND ADMINISTRATION

munity and other area groups? Would a group, from either the parish or the community, be permitted to use the parish hall or other facilities to present a controversial speaker or program? Have members of other churches used the parish facilities? Give examples. Should their use of parish facilities be actively sought? Do you think Christ would be pleased with the use made of parish facilities?

Act

Write below any suggested action or actions from your discussion:

After evaluating the policy on the use of parish facilities, might a subcommittee be formed to improve the policy, make recommendations to the council board, or perhaps create a continuing service project for the promotion and effective use of parish facilities?

Might leaders of the community life and social committees be consulted on the needs for meeting facilities that they have discovered through their work? Write your assignments here:

Are members of the parish permitted to use parish facilities, at no cost or a reasonable fee, for family reunions, wedding receptions, anniversaries, etc.? Could this possibility be investigated?

Fifth Action Meeting

See

Report and discuss all actions taken since the last meeting.

Review your sources of income in the last annual report and in the budget for the current fiscal year. Discuss. Are a good number of groups and a great amount of time spent in raising funds in your worshipping community?

Do you use the envelope system? What is your reaction to it? Do you know how other parishioners feel about the system?

Are you raising enough money to meet your full budget? Are you raising additional money so that parishioners might express their obligations to the poor, the diocese, the universal Church?

Do you have a program now so that your parish contributes to the support of a missionary, pays the living expenses of a PAVLA or Extension volunteer in Latin America or this country, helps support an inner-city parish, or has "adopted" a poor parish somewhere in the world? List all such activities that your parish is presently engaged in:

Are parishioners told personally about the financial needs of the parish, the varied charitable works of the parish, and then requested to make a just and charitable contribution? What information do they receive when they are given their weekly envelopes? Is there a follow-up program of education and information to persons who use the weekly envelopes? May parishioners elect to contribute in any other way?

Judge

Discuss what Christ's plan for your financial program might be for your worshipping community.

Act

Write below the action or actions that might be suggested by your discussion:

Is it possible that your worshipping community might be able to end all fund-raising events if a program of personal contact and explanation of parish obligations were undertaken? Could a subcommittee review the budget, see what would be needed to achieve this goal, evaluate whether it would be practical, and report to the full committee? Write your assignments below:

Should the finance and administration committee review the possibility of follow-up interviews with newly registered members of the worshipping community to explain the financial program of the parish and solicit the new members' support?

Plan your next meeting now. Set a date, time, and place. Be sure to ask for action reports. What topic will be discussed? Might you evaluate the progress of your committee? Are committee members active and enthusiastic? Are friendships forming and concerns for each other and the worshipping community expressed? Is the committee growing? Can you project the financial and administrative needs for the coming year? Write your plan of action here: